Grammar Made Simple

Grade 4

Written by Sara Freeman
Illustrated by Mike Denman

FS123303 Grammar Made Simple Grade 4
All rights reserved. Printed in the U.S.A.
Copyright © 2000 Frank Schaffer Publications
23740 Hawthorne Blvd.
Torrance, CA 90505

D1495536

Table
of Contents

Introduction

Teaching children to speak and write effectively is a key component of a well-rounded education. Grammar is the cornerstone of that teaching. Children's questions show they want to know the how and why of oral and written communication.

Which "to" should I write?

What does "Sr." mean?

ow do I write a thank-you note?

Why can't I say "Me and Kelly . . . "?

Frank Schaffer's *Grammar Made Simple Grade 4* is designed to give students a strong foundation in language skills. The book contains teacher ideas for whole-class activities, group activities, and partner activities. In addition, there are reproducible student pages designed for practicing specific skills.

There are four sections in this book: Sentences, Parts of Speech, Usage, and Mechanics (Capitalization and Punctuation). Each section starts with a basic teacher review of the concepts included in that segment. Because the topics of each section are interrelated, you may choose to introduce them in any order. Let your students' strengths and weaknesses guide you in selecting which topics to focus on.

Many adults can sense if their writing is correct because it "sounds right." Therefore, a multitude of oral language activities is included to help students speak correctly and develop an ear for correct grammar. This will also help develop your students' confidence in speaking as well as make the concepts come alive for them.

Grammar instruction does not have to be dull and dry. *Grammar Made Simple Grade 4* helps you engage different styles of learners in fun and meaningful activities. This resource not only makes it easy for you to teach grammar— it makes it easy for your students to learn!

Sentences

Just as the dollar is the basic unit of currency in the United States, the sentence is the basic unit in writing. Learning the structure of sentences, as well as the different types, will help students communicate in speaking and in writing.

SENTENCE MIX-UP

The words in a sentence need to be in an order that makes sense. This activity lets students practice puttin sentence words in order. Divide the class into groups of four. Have each student find a short sentence (five eight words) from a book and write the words on paper in alphabetical order. Example: *bike his Jason jumped off.* In turn, let each student show and read aloud his or her mixed-up sentence to the group. The remaining group members write the sentence correctly on their own papers. You can adapt this idea for advanced students by having them choose longer or more complex sentences.

WHAT'S MISSING?

Copy onto the chalkboard a three-sentence paragraph from a book you've been reading. Omit end punctuation and do not capitalize the first word in each sentence. Challenge students to read the passage and figure out the sentences. Invite students to come to the chalkboard to make corrections. Follow up by letting students create on paper a similar sentence-deciphering activity for a classmate to edit.

ANIMAL CAPTIONS

Skim through nature magazines, cutting out interesting photos of animals. Glue each photo to a piece of tagboard, and laminate it to make it sturdier. Give pairs of students an animal picture card to share. Challenge the pairs to write four different captions or thought bubbles to match what their animal is saying or thinking. Direct them to use complete sentences. Invite pairs to share their favorite captions with the class.

Our favorite caption was, "I think I'm in trouble!"

LOOKING AT SENTENCES

...nd opening sentences or paragraphs from different books that "hook" the reader—either through vivid ...ages or hints about upcoming events. Suggestions:

...*e Best Christmas Pageant Ever* by Barbara Robinson (HarperCollins, 1972) uses humor to introduce the Herdmans—the "worst kids in the history of the world."

...*e Chocolate Touch* by Patrick Skene Catling (Dell, 1996) creates suspense in the first two paragraphs by stating the main character usually behaved well but should have behaved better.

...*one Fox* by John Reynolds Gardiner (Harper Trophy, 1983) creates an easy-to-picture image of a child's grandfather whose normal behavior has changed.

...*e True Story of the 3 Little Pigs* by Jon Scieszka (Viking, 1989) makes readers question what they thought they already knew.

...*ill You Sign Here, John Hancock?* by Jean Fritz (Putnam, 1982) uses a friendly style to introduce Boston in colonial times.

...ead aloud the passages. Discuss the sentences and ask students questions such as these: *Do the sentences ...lp you picture a scene in your head? Do they make you want to read more? How?* Help students as needed ...recognize picturesque words, unexpected ideas, or humorous phrases that entice the reader.

...en direct students to skim through five books, comparing the opening sentences, paragraphs, or pages. ...ave them choose which one they think has the best lead. Tell students to write the title of the book, copy ...opening, and write a paragraph explaining what they liked about it. You can extend this activity into a ...eative-writing project by challenging students to write opening paragraphs of their own.

SENTENCE ADD-ON

...t small groups play this sentence-building game. All ...ch group needs is a pencil and a sheet of paper. One ...rson begins by writing a two-word sentence that ...s a subject and a verb. Example: *Fido barks.* That ...rson passes the paper to the next player. Each ...ayer in turn adds one or two words to the sentence, ...riting the new version below. Players can help each ...her with spelling, punctuation, and capitalization ...ly—not with ideas. Play continues until a player can't ...ink of any more words to add. The stumped player ...egins the next round with a new two-word sentence.

> *Fido barks.*
> *Fido barks loudly.*
> *My dog Fido barks loudly.*
> *My sweet dog Fido barks loudly.*
> *My sweet dog Fido barks loudly at night.*
> *My sweet dog Fido never barks loudly at night.*

SILLY SUBJECTS, PREPOSTEROUS PREDICATES

Make a class set of mix-and-match subjects and predicates. Give each student two index cards. For the first card, have students make up two silly subjects. Direct each student to write a singular subject on one side and a plural subject on the back. Have them capitalize the first letters of the first words. For the second card, have students make up two preposterous predicates. Tell students to write predicates for singular subjects on one side and predicates for plural subjects on the backs. Direct them to place ending punctuation at the ends of their predicates. The predicates do not need to match the themes of the subjects. Here are ideas for using the cards:

> My sister's pet caterpillar named Fred

> likes to do back flips in the pool.

> Fourteen crying babies in stinky diapers

> play computer games at midnight.

1. Read aloud a subject card. Have each student write it and make up a predicate to finish the sentence.

2. Read aloud a predicate card. Have each student make up a subject for it and write the complete sentenc[e]

3. Pass out a subject card to each student. Call on students to read aloud their cards and identify the simp[le] subjects. Example: *Several four-eyed, earless <u>monsters</u>*

4. Pass out a predicate card to each student. Call on students to read aloud their cards and identify the simple predicates (verbs). Example: *angrily <u>marched</u> under my bed.*

5. Pass out a subject card and predicate card to each student. Have students read both sides to decide which subject goes with which predicate.

6. Have students work in groups of four. Pass out four of each card to every group. Tell groups to read among themselves the different sentence combinations. Let individuals write and illustrate their favorit[e] wacky sentences.

COMPOUND SUBJECTS

Let students know that some sentences have compound subjects—two or more simple subjects. Examples: <u>Picasso</u> and <u>Monet</u> are my favorite artists. <u>Steve</u>, <u>Liz</u>, and their <u>cousin</u> went rock climbing last week. Next, find a book with sentences that have a variety of subjects. Read aloud a sentence. Have students decide how many simple subjects there are in the sentence and hold up that many fingers. Call on a student to name the simple subject(s). As an alternative, you may want every student to write the simple subject(s). After you have done this activity several times, tell students to keep their eyes closed as they raise their fingers. You can then see at a glance which students grasp the concept and which need additional practice.

DECLARE

irect the class to stand. Tell students that to be able to sit down, they will need to give a statement about emselves or something they observe. Examples: *I am wearing a blue shirt. Our pet hamster is sleeping. arisa and Lauren like working together.* Call on students in random order. You can make the activity more n by listing some characters on the chalkboard, such as a snooty know-it-all, a weeping man, or a Southern elle. Invite students to make their statements using the voice of one of the characters.

MEASURING QUESTIONS

ere's a fun way to mix math with terrogative sentences. Give pairs f students rulers or measuring pes. Challenge them to write five uestions that relate to body easurements. Have pairs measure find the answers and then write em as complete sentences. Ask r a volunteer to help you model a mple question and answer.

Are our feet the same length?

Mrs. Campbell's feet are two inches longer than Mario's feet.

WHO'S GIVING ORDERS?

each or review with students that imperative sentences are commands. Explain to students that imperative entences often omit the subject and begin with a verb. If there is no subject, it is understood to be *you.* xample: *Give me that ball. (You) give me that ball.* Tell students to pretend that something wacky has appened at home or at school. They are now in charge and are giving commands to adults. Have each student raw a scene depicting the funny things that might occur, then write five commands that match the scene.

STEP-BY-STEP

irections are one of the most common applications of imperative entences that students encounter. Find an art project book that you njoy. Read aloud the directions to one of the projects. Direct students to sten for the words that start the sentences. (Most will be verbs.) Elicit hose beginning words from students and write them on the chalkboard. hen choose an art project you have done recently. Display various tages of the project to jog students' memories of the steps involved. hallenge students to work alone or with partners to write directions or the project. Tell them to use commands in their directions.

READ WITH EXPRESSION

Gather multiple copies of the picture book *How Joe the Bear and Sam the Mouse Got Together* by Beatrice Schenk de Regniers (Lothrop, Lee and Shepard, 1965). This story tells how a big bear and a little mouse become friends even though they like different things. The story is told through conversations that will provide your students with the opportunity to read declarative, imperative, interrogative, and exclamatory sentences with expression. Read aloud the first few pages to engage students in the story and to model how to use a low voice for the bear and a high voice for the mouse. Then give pairs of students copies of the book. Let each student choose a part—Joe or Sam—and read the book aloud using expression. Since this will be noisy, you may want to do this activity outside where pairs can spread out. (If you do not have enough copies of the book, have students work in groups of four, switching roles. Two students read while the other two listen for different types of sentences.) Finish with a class discussion about how different types of sentences are read. Sample discussion questions: *How does your voice change when you are asking a question? Which sentences showed emotion? How did you know? How did you read them?*

Homework

Listen Up!

Try this homework activity after you have taught different types of sentences—statements, questions, commands, and exclamations. Begin by acting out a phone conversation:

Hello! . . . This is she. . . . No, I'm not interested. . . . No. . . . Thank you anyway. Good-bye.

Ask students who they think just called you— your best friend, a phone solicitor, or the President of the United States. Then ask them if the person on the other end asked you any questions and how they could tell.

For homework, direct students to get permission to listen to one side of a parent's phone conversation. To make sure parents and students understand the assignment, you may want to explain it in a note like the one to the left. Challenge students to infer what types of sentences are being said and to explain how they could tell. Hold a class discussion afterward to discuss the results. You may want to follow up the assignment with the page 60 writing activity "Silent Conversation."

Dear Parents,

We have been studying different types of sentences. With your permission, for homework, your child would like to listen to your side of a short phone conversation sometime this week. Naturally, it should be a conversation you would not mind your child hearing—ordering a pizza, calling to say hello to a grandparent, setting up a play date for kids.

As your child listens to both the words you speak and your intonation, he or she will be inferring the types of sentences the other person is using: statements, questions, commands, or exclamations. After the conversation, you may want to talk over with your child what he or she heard and inferred.

If you do not want your child to participate in this activity, he or she can write one side of an imaginary phone conversation as an alternative homework assignment.

Thank you!

ANIMAL RIDDLES

Use student interest in animals to teach how to form compound sentences that are connected by the word *but*. Begin by writing this riddle on the chalkboard. Invite students to write the answer at their desks (a rattlesnake). Next, ask students what the riddle clues each have in common. (It is not ____, but it _____.) Point out how each sentence could be two separate short sentences. Example: *It is not a fish. It does have scales.* Discuss how a lot of short, choppy sentences can sound boring. Explain how the word *but* can join two sentences that have similarities and differences. Ask students what punctuation mark comes before the word *but* when it connects two sentences (a comma).

Direct students to follow these steps to write their own animal riddles. Post the riddles on a bulletin board for students to read and solve.

. Choose an animal.

. List characteristics of that animal.

. Think of another animal that shares each characteristic.

. Write sentence clues for each characteristic that follows this pattern: *It is not a/an ____, but it _____.* Use your easiest clues last.

. End the riddle with this question: *What is it?*

. Draw your answer on the back of the paper.

> *It is not a dog, but it does shed.*
>
> *It is not an owl, but it does eat mice.*
>
> *It is not a fish, but it does have scales.*
>
> *It is not a black widow spider, but it is poisonous.*
>
> *It is not a jackrabbit, but it does live in the desert.*
>
> *It is not a frog, but it is cold-blooded.*
>
> *It is not a turtle, but it is a reptile.*
>
> *It is not an alligator, but it is long.*
>
> *It is not a baby, but it does have a rattle.*
>
> *What is it?*

AND THEN AND THEN AND THEN . . .

Alexander and the Terrible, Horrible, No Good, Very Bad Day by Judith Viorst (Atheneum, 1977) has classic examples of rambling sentences. Read aloud the opening page. Be dramatic in needing to take a breath at the end of that 62-word sentence! Point out to students that to be humorous, the writer deliberately made the sentence too long. Explain that in most writing, sentences that go on and on and on need to be broken into two or more smaller sentences. Finish reading the book to your class. Then have students think of another series of terrible, horrible, no good, very bad things that could have happened to Alexander. Tell students to write those events as Alexander would—in one long rambling sentence. Then have them rewrite the sentence correctly, breaking it into several smaller sentences.

All About Penguins

A **sentence** is a group of words that tells a complete thought.

Help Hannah fix this writing piece about penguins. Find and underline the groups of words that are not complete sentences. They are missing either the part of the sentence that tells whom or what the sentence is about, or the part that tells what something does or is. Write them correctly below.

Penguins are my favorite birds. I like the way they waddle. So cute!

Penguins cannot fly. They have flippers instead of wings. Are very good swimmers and divers.

Many different kinds of penguins. Emperor penguins are the largest. They can be four feet tall and weigh close to 100 pounds. Fairy penguins are the smallest. They are a little more than one foot tall. Only weigh about two pounds.

Someday I hope to visit Antarctica. Then see my favorite birds.

1. _____

_____

2. _____

_____

3. _____

_____

4. _____

_____

5. _____

FS123303 Grammar Made Simple Grade 4 ■ © Frank Schaffer Publications, Inc.

Make Your Own Sentences

A **sentence** is a group of words that tells a complete thought.

Look at these pictures. Use the words given and add some of your own to make a sentence. Begin each sentence with a capital letter and end it with a period.

Example:

The tiny frog was too scared
to jump off the lily pad.

| frog |
| lily pad |
| jump |

1. _____

_____

_____

| paint |
| needs |
| boy |

2. _____

_____

_____

| goal |
| girl |
| soccer |

3. _____

_____

_____

| know |
| dinosaur |
| tail |

4. _____

_____

_____

| plant |
| garden |
| summer |

5. _____

_____

_____

| snail |
| race |
| slow |

Amusement Park Fun

The **subject** is the part of a sentence that tells whom or what the sentence is about.
The **predicate** is the part of a sentence that tells what the subject is or does.

Subject   Predicate

The roller coaster at Funway Park   *is really big.*
Mark and Amber   *like to ride it.*

Pretend you and your friends are at an amusement park.
Read each sentence. Write a subject or predicate to finish it.

Missing Subjects

1. _____ are more
   fun than the bumper cars.

2. _____ is the best ride at our
   amusement park.

3. _____ had to wait in line for an hour to go on the log ride.

4. _____ did not want to be in the front seat.

5. _____ bought some popcorn for all of us to share.

Missing Predicates

6. The kids who were standing in line in front of us _____

   _____.

7. My friends and I _____.

8. The woman at the Coin Toss booth _____

   _____.

9. My parents _____

   _____.

10. Our day at the park _____

   _____.

FS123303 Grammar Made Simple Grade 4 ■ © Frank Schaffer Publications, Inc

Community Food Share

The **complete subject** is all the words in a sentence that tell whom or what the sentence is about.

The **simple subject** is the one main word that tells whom or what the sentence is about.

Read each sentence. Underline the complete subject. Write the simple subject on the line.

children   <u>The children in our class</u> wanted to do a service project.

We   <u>We</u> voted on different ideas.

project   <u>The project I thought of</u> got the most votes.

_____ 1. We chose to hold a food drive at our school to help the
Community Food Share program.

_____ 2. That program gives away food to people who need it.

_____ 3. One group of kids made posters about the food drive to hang all
over school.

_____ 4. Another group spoke about the food drive at a school assembly.

_____ 5. The group I was in wrote a note to send home to families.

_____ 6. Kids in all the different classes brought in cans and boxes of food
from home.

_____ 7. Our class sorted all the food.

_____ 8. Our parents helped deliver the food we collected.

_____ 9. We took a field trip to the Community Food Share building.

_____ 10. The people at Community Food Share showed us where they
store the food.

_____ 11. They were thankful for all that our class and school did.

_____ 12. Our class felt great that we had made a difference in our
community!

The Slumber Party

The **complete predicate** is all the words in a sentence that tell what the subject is or does.

The **simple predicate** is the one main word that tells what the subject is or does.

Read each sentence. Underline the complete predicate. Write the simple predicate on the line.

had — My friend and I <u>had an Egyptian-theme slumber party</u>.

was — It <u>was really fun</u>!

started — Jenna and I <u>started planning the party by reading lots of books about ancient Egypt</u>.

1. _____ We made invitations that were shaped like cat mummies.
2. _____ I drew the pictures of the cats.
3. _____ Jenna wrote the party details.
4. _____ Our friends wore white clothes and gold jewelry to the party.
5. _____ Some of us had black wigs.
6. _____ Both men and women in ancient Egypt wore makeup.
7. _____ We put on eye makeup to look more Egyptian.
8. _____ My friend Emily read aloud her book *Cleopatra*.
9. _____ Everyone acted out the parts.
10. _____ I needed to change my clothes to be Mark Antony.
11. _____ Our friend Maria brought a stamp kit she has of hieroglyphics.
12. _____ Hieroglyphics are picture symbols that Egyptians used for writing.
13. _____ We stamped our names on paper.
14. _____ My friends and I were hungry by then.
15. _____ Everybody snacked on foods that were not Egyptian!
16. _____ We finally went to bed at 1:00 a.m.

FS123303 Grammar Made Simple Grade 4 ■ © Frank Schaffer Publications, Inc.

$\int$ ports Day

Sometimes you can combine two short sentences that have the same subject or the same predicate into one longer sentence. You may need to change a few words.

Same subject:

Lisa will show how to throw a baseball.
Lisa will show how to catch a baseball.
Lisa will show how to throw and catch a baseball.

Same predicate:

Bryce is drawing a poster about track and field.
Amy is drawing a poster about track and field.
Bryce and Amy are drawing posters about track and field.

Read each set of sentences. Write them as one sentence.

1. Marco will demonstrate yo-yo tricks.
   Kelsey will demonstrate yo-yo tricks.

   _____

   _____

2. Laura is teaching how to dribble a soccer ball.
   Laura is teaching how to pass a soccer ball.

   _____

   _____

3. Todd will bring his skates.
   Todd will bring his helmet.

   _____

   _____

4. Ryan is making up a game about famous athletes.
   Maggie is making up a game about famous athletes.

   _____

   _____

An Amazing Dog

A **statement** is a sentence that tells something.
It begins with a capital letter and ends with a period (**.**).

A **question** is a sentence that asks something.
It begins with a capital letter and ends with a question mark (**?**).

Pretend Anna is interviewing Chatty Chow, a talking dog. What questions would she ask?
What statements would he make for answers? Fill in the captions.

Oh, My Gosh!

An **exclamation** is a sentence that shows strong feeling.
It may tell a complete thought, or it may just be a word or phrase.
It begins with a capital letter and ends with an exclamation mark (**!**).
Examples:

I can't believe that happened!
What a day!
Great!

Look at each scene. Write three exclamations the person might make.

1. _____
2. _____
3. _____
   _____

1. _____
2. _____
3. _____
   _____

1. _____
2. _____
3. _____
   _____

1. _____
2. _____
3. _____
   _____

The Bossy Basketball

A **command** is a sentence that tells someone to do something.
It begins with a capital letter and ends with a period (.).
Some commands begin with a verb. The missing subject is understood to be *you*.
Examples:

> *Matthew, come here.*
> *(You) Tell me about your game.*

Pretend Matthew's basketball has come to life. It is giving him commands.
Read Matthew's responses. Write the commands the basketball gave him.
You may add a statement to go with each command also.

Basketball: _____

_____

_____

_____

Matthew: But I don't want to!

Basketball: _____

_____

Matthew: I'm sorry.

Basketball: _____

_____

Matthew: Why are you being so bossy?

Basketball: _____

_____

Matthew: Yes, Your Highness. I will do what you say.

 FS123303 Grammar Made Simple Grade 4 ▪ © Frank Schaffer Publications, Inc

Magnet Fun

Read each sentence.
If it is a statement, write **S** and add the missing period.
If it is a question, write **Q** and add the missing question mark.
If it is a command, write **C** and add the missing period.
If it is an exclamation, write **E** and add the missing exclamation mark.

<u>E</u>   Yay, no science test today **!**

<u>Q</u>   What are we doing instead **?**

<u>S</u>   We are doing a magnet experiment **.**

<u>C</u>   Go get the magnets for our group, please **.**

____ 1. Which kind of magnets do you want

____ 2. Mario, check if there are horseshoe magnets

____ 3. I'll go get the iron filings

____ 4. What do we do now

____ 5. Put a magnet on the desk, place a paper over it, and sprinkle iron filings on it

____ 6. Look at the patterns

____ 7. Wow

____ 8. Can you tell where the poles are

____ 9. I think they are at the ends of the magnet because
there are clumps of filings there

____ 10. Let's do two magnets together

____ 11. I'll lift the paper and pour the filings back into the jar

____ 12. Oh, no

____ 13. What's wrong

____ 14. I spilled all the filings

____ 15. Use the magnet to pick them up

Parts of Speech

Parts of speech are categories of words. The categories are based on how words are used in a sentence. Some words can fit into more than one category. For example, *look* can be a verb or a noun. *Mr. Sanchez, look at me. My sister gave me a strange look.* In English, there are eight parts of speech:

1. **Nouns** name a person, place, thing, or idea. (*girl, Georgia, computer, honesty*)

2. **Pronouns** take the place of nouns. (*she, it, them, us*)

3. **Verbs** show action or a state of being. (*skate, played, is, were*)

4. **Adjectives** describe a noun or pronoun. (*hungry, old, better*)

5. **Adverbs** tell about a verb, adjective, or another adverb. (*quietly, very*)

6. **Prepositions** show the position or relationship between a noun and another word. (*under, next to, inside*)

7. **Conjunctions** connect words or phrases. (*and, but, or*)

8. **Interjections** show emotion. (*wow, oops, oh!*)

HEADLINE HUNT

Partner Activity

Newspapers are a great resource when studying parts of speech (and many other topics). Students can mark them up, cut them apart, and then recycle them. Here's an easy activity to get you started. Choose a part of speech, such as verbs. Give pairs of students sections of the newspaper. (They could be different sections and different days.) Have the pairs hunt through headlines and circle all the verbs they can find in five minutes. Invite pairs to read aloud the verbs they circled. Involve the rest of the class by having them vote thumbs up (yes) or thumbs down (no) on whether the words being read are verbs.

MAD LIBS

Class Activity

Mad Libs (Price/Stern/Sloan, 1986) are a quick and delightful way to teach, practice, or review parts of speech. You can purchase them through a bookstore or school book club. A silly paragraph or story is written with several blanks in it. Each blank is identified with the missing part of speech (plural noun, verb, adverb . . .). You first ask for the missing parts of speech from your students and write their suggestions in the blanks: *Who can give me a plural noun?* Once all blanks are filled in, you read aloud the silly story. *Mad Libs* also work well for pairs or small groups. Once your students become "Master Mad Libbers," challenge them to write their own, focusing on the parts of speech you want them to practice.

100 PEOPLE

Tell students that a noun names a person, place, thing, or idea. Explain that for this activity the class will be focusing on people. Give a few examples of nouns that name people—boy, grandmother, dancer, neighbor. Then let students pick partners. Challenge pairs to come up with lists of 100 nouns that name people. Tell pairs that the nouns cannot be names, such as Eric or Mrs. Henderson.

Homework

What's in the Drawer?

Nouns are everywhere—even in a kitchen drawer. Tell students their homework assignment is to choose a kitchen drawer and to list all the items in it. They may need to get some help from a sibling or adult to name some of the utensils. Encourage them to use adjectives as needed to distinguish between different items. Example: *rubber spatula, metal spatula, long grill spatula*. At school, label a long banner "Kitchen Nouns A–Z" and write the letters of the alphabet across it. Invite students to copy utensil names from their lists to the banner. Tell students not to duplicate any items.

CREATE A MAP

Invite children to imagine a wonderful island just for kids. Ask them to describe what might be on the island. Let children sketch and label maps to match their own ideas. Direct students to think of names for their islands and 10 different places on them. Remind students that names of places are proper nouns and should begin with a capital letter. Let children show their completed maps to the class or a group.

DESCRIBE MY CHARACTER

Have students work with partners for this activity. One partner makes up a character name and writes it correctly, capitalizing the first letter of each word, initial, or title. The partner then makes up and gives an oral description of the character. Partners switch roles and repeat the activity several times. Encourage students to keep the lists of names in their creative writing folders to use in their writing.

HUNTING FOR PLURALS, PART I

This activity lets children work as a team to find plurals in a book. Divide the class into groups of three. Direct each group to select a two-page passage in a chapter book. Read these job descriptions and tell groups to choose parts among themselves:

1. The Reader slowly reads aloud the pages, pausing when plurals are called out.

2. The Caller calls out a plural noun when he or she sees it or hears it being read.

3. The Scribe writes down each plural noun on a sheet of paper.

Model for students how to do each job. Then give groups 15-20 minutes to complete the activity.

HUNTING FOR PLURALS, PART II

Follow-up the earlier activity with a teacher-directed lesson on classifying the plural nouns. As you do this lesson, make a plurals rule chart that students can refer to later.

1. Tell students that most words are made plural by adding the letter *s* to the ends. Give them the example *book-books*. Have groups read through their lists and draw stars beside each word that was made plural by adding only *s*. Call on each group to say one or more of their starred words and to give the singular forms.

2. Next, have groups look for words that are made plural by adding *es* to the end, such as *dish-dishes*. Direct groups to mark those words with checks and to underline the two letters that comes before the *es* Call on each group to say all of their checked words, naming the underlined letters. Keep a running list of those letters. Use your students' words to point out that words ending in *ch, sh, s, x,* and *z* are made plural by adding the *es* ending.

3. Then direct groups to look for plurals ending in *ies* and to mark diamonds next to them. Give them the example *penny-pennies*. Invite groups to name their diamond words and to give the singular form for each. Explain that words ending with a *consonant-y*, such as *penny*, are made plural by changing the *y* to *i* and adding *es*. Words that end with a *vowel-y*, such as *day*, are made plural simply by adding *s*.

4. End by having groups circle the remaining words on their lists. Ask each group to read the words and give the singular form of each. Explain that some words are irregular plurals, such as *child-children* or *moose-moose*. Make a wall chart of irregular plurals and invite students to add to it throughout the year.

ANIMAL PLURALS

Many animal names have irregular plurals. Read aloud picture book versions of the Noah/Great Flood story, such as *Aardvarks, Disembark!* by Ann Jonas (Greenwillow, 1990) or *Llama and the Great Flood* by Ellen Alexander (Crowell, 1989). For a follow-up bulletin board, draw a boat shape in the center of the board and label it "Animal Plurals." Brainstorm a list of animals, and record the list on a sheet of paper. Let students sign up to draw three or more pairs of animals. Each animal pair should be labeled with the correct plural form and then placed on the bulletin board.

WHOSE IS IT?

Ask students to bring in toy- or craft-store inserts from the newspaper. Have students cut out pictures of appealing items and paste them to pieces of paper. Next, direct students to think of someone who would like each item, pretend that person has it, and write a label to match. Model for students how to write an apostrophe s ('s) to show possession. Example: *Mary Beth's candle kit*

PICTURE THIS

Teach or review with students how nouns are made possessive. Draw a sketch to match each example:

an apostrophe s ('s) is added to the end of singular nouns (*girl—the girl's books*)

an apostrophe (') is added to the end of plural nouns that end with s (*boys—the boys' books*)

an apostrophe s ('s) is added to the end of plural nouns that do not end with s (*children—the children's books*)

Then invite a student to come to the board and write a phrase with a possessive noun for the rest of the class to illustrate at their desks. Examples: *Bobby's pencils, the dinosaurs' spikes, the women's skis.* The student who writes the phrase should be able to explain whether or not the other students' pictures are correct.

HE, SHE, HIM, HER

Read aloud a passage from a chapter book. Replace all pronouns with the noun they stand for. Example: *Mike's grandmother gave Mike a new bike for Mike's birthday. Mike walked over to Mike's new bike. Mike put on Mike's helmet . . .* Ask students how they think the story sounds. Explain that pronouns take the places of nouns. Pronouns add variety to writing so the same nouns aren't repeated over and over again. Write a list of nouns found on the page you were reading. Ask students to give pronouns that could take the places of those nouns. Explain that how a noun is used within a sentence determines which pronoun to use. Challenge students to name other pronouns they can think of. Then have students look in books for paragraphs with five or more pronouns. Direct them to copy the paragraphs once and then to rewrite them, replacing all pronouns with the nouns they stand for.

VERB TRAINS

Teach or review that most verbs are action words. Brainstorm a quick list—*sing, look, play, write, dribble, trick, breathe*. Then model for students how to make verb trains. Write a verb on the chalkboard, and underline the last letter. Have a volunteer come to the chalkboard and write a verb that begins with the underlined letter. Repeat this process with different volunteers until you have a five-word train. Let students work with partners to make their own verb trains. Challenge the class to see who can make the longest train.

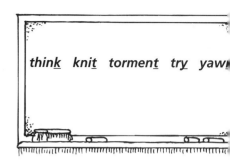

thin<u>k</u> kni<u>t</u> tormen<u>t</u> tr<u>y</u> yaw<u>

SEEING, SAYING, DOING, PLAYING

Share the book *Seeing, Saying, Doing, Playing* by Taro Gomi (Chronicl 1991) with your students. This colorful book shows fun busy scenes of children and adults, each labeled with an *ing* verb. For example, in a pool scene, the verb accompanying the child at the end of the high div is *reconsidering*. Invite students to color their own busy scenes on large sheets of blank paper. Then direct them to label all people and animals with *ing* verbs. Encourage students to use a thesaurus or dictionary to find interesting verbs and to check the spelling of verbs.

FILL IN THE VERBS

Let students compare their choice of verbs with those of an author. Choose a descriptive passage from a picture book. For example, read aloud the first page of *Stellaluna* by Janell Cannon (Harcourt Brace, 1993) to introduce the story. Write the second page of the story on the chalkboard or overhead projector, or type it on paper and make copies for students. Omit most or all of the verbs from the passage you copy and put writin lines in their places. Direct students to think of verbs that would fit the context. Invite students to read aloud the passage using their verbs. Then read the actual passage as the author wrote it. Compare the verb choices and the images each created.

EXPLORE THE THESAURUS

Divide the class into small groups. Give each group a thesaurus and a piece of butcher paper. Assign each group one of these verbs to look up in the thesaurus: *bother, break, cry, eat, hate, laugh, like, make, quiet, run, scare, shout, walk, want.* Direct groups to write their words in the center of their papers and to surround them with the synonyms they find. Each synonym should have a written description that explains the word's meaning, especially how it differs slightly from the central word. Encourage groups to illustrate some of their verbs. Let each group explain their finished word charts. Post the charts on a wall for student to refer to when sprucing up their own writing.

VERBS OF BEING

Explain that not all verbs are action words. Write these verbs of being on the chalkboard: *am, is, are, was, were*. Give a few sample sentences for each verb. Examples: *I am tired. Misha and Rachel were at the library.* Then have students work in groups of three to do this oral activity. One student in each group chooses a verb of being, such as *was*. The second group member names a subject to match and repeats the verb: *Michael Jordan was.* The third group member completes the sentence using the subject and verb: *Michael Jordan was the greatest basketball player ever.* Tell students to take turns so that each person gets several chances to choose the verb, name the subject, and finish the sentence.

WHAT DID YOU DO YESTERDAY?

Mix math with grammar in this activity. Have each student draw 10 clocks across the top of a large sheet of paper. The first clock should show the time the student woke up and the final clock should show the time the student began getting ready for bed. The clocks in between should be in chronological order showing a variety of times during the day. Challenge students to list five past-tense verbs under each clock, telling what they did at that time. Explain that they cannot repeat a verb on the page. If students choose to write phrases, have them underline the verbs. Let students read their pages to partners before turning in the assignment. Partners can help each other look for incorrect or repeated verbs.

<u>woke</u> up

<u>reached</u> for the alarm clock

<u>pushed</u> down the button

<u>rolled</u> out of bed

<u>stumbled</u> to the bathroom

THINK I THOUGHT

Read aloud Marvin Terban's delightful language book *I Think I Thought and Other Tricky Verbs* (Clarion, 1984). It blends rhyming couplets and whimsical art to present irregular past tense verbs, as in this example: *Stingray sings songs to submarines. Sawfish sang softly to sardines.* Make copies of the page 38 reproducible "Draw, Drew, Drawn" to give to students as a resource. Challenge pairs of students to write and illustrate their own present and past tense rhyming couplets. Ask each pair to choose their favorite set and compile those into a class book.

ADJECTIVE OPPOSITES

Teach or review that adjectives are describing words. Name an adjective, such as *young*, and have the class call out its opposite (*old*). Do several words and let the class continue to call out the opposites. Then have each student work with a partner. Tell students to list as many pairs of adjective opposites as they can, with each being worth two points. Challenge the students to make lists that total more than 100 points.

MAKE A COLOR MINI-BOOK

Colors are frequently used adjectives. Help students expand their writing by learning new color words. Begin by gathering large sheets of construction paper in these basic colors: yellow, orange, red, blue, green, purple, brown, and black. To make writing more visible, tape white writing paper onto the black sheet. Brainstorm a list of color words students already know, and write them on the closest-matching color sheets. Challenge students to find additional color words on their own. (Crayon boxes and clothing catalogs are good sources of words—*charcoal*, *plum*, *cinnamon*, *kelly green*, *dusty rose*.) Then help students follow the directions below to make their own color mini-books. Each student will need a blank sheet of paper, scissors, and one rubber band.

1. Fold a blank sheet of paper in half widthwise twice and unfold it.

2. Fold it in half lengthwise and unfold it.

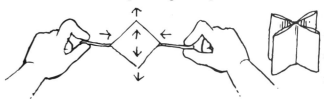

3. Fold it in half widthwise once again. Cut halfway across the middle fold line. Unfold the paper to see the center slit.

 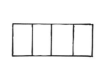

4. Fold the paper in half lengthwise once again.

5. Hold the ends and push them toward the center to make a plus-sign shape.

6. Stretch a rubber band around the center to make a book spine. Push the pages together to make an eight-page book. Label the cover.

7. Choose seven colors to write on the other pages. Write interesting color words under each of the main headings. Color samples if you want to show the differences.

 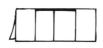

FS123303 Grammar Made Simple Grade 4 ▪ © Frank Schaffer Publications, In

SENSORY ADJECTIVES

Poetry is full of wonderful adjectives (and nouns and verbs and adverbs!). Adjectives help the reader or listener understand how something or someone looks, feels, sounds, smells, or tastes. Read aloud poems to your students and have them listen for adjectives that evoke the senses. Here are some suggestions from the poetry book *Sing a Song of Popcorn* (Scholastic, 1988):

"I Have a Lion" by Karla Kuskin
"Grandpa Bear's Lullaby" by Jane Yolen
"The Bat" by Theodore Roethke
"I Heard a Bird Sing" by Oliver Herford
"April Rain Song" by Langston Hughes
"Knoxville, Tennessee" by Nikki Giovanni
"Night Creature" by Lilian Moore
"Winter Moon" by Langston Hughes

Follow up by having students find poems to share with the class. Direct students to copy the poems in their best handwriting, underlining their favorite adjectives. Post the poems on a bulletin board. You may want students to add pictures to accompany their poems. For example, a child might cut raindrops from foil to highlight the phrase "silver liquid drops" in Langston Hughes's poem "April Rain Song."

SAD, SADDER, SADDEST

Call three students to the front of the class and give them an adjective, such as *sad*. Have them each recite a sentence and act it out to show the meaning of the adjective in its basic, comparative, and superlative forms: *sad, sadder, saddest*. Here are some adjectives to choose from: *quiet, silly, short, tall, smart, funny, happy, sad, hungry, grumpy, kind, old, clean, noisy, slow, hot.* Have the remaining students write the adjectives at their desks. During this time you can also teach a mini-lesson on spelling patterns that relates to doubling the final consonant or changing the *y* to *i* before adding the endings. For a tactile version of this activity, have students work in groups of three. Give each group balls of play dough. Have them use the dough at their desks to make simple models of adjectives, such as *big, bigger, biggest*.

BEAUTIFULLEST?

Tell students that this morning you saw the "beautifullest" sunrise. If no students catch your mistake, ask them if *beautifullest* is a word. Challenge students to give the correct form—*most beautiful.* Explain that some multisyllable adjectives use the word *more* when comparing two nouns and *most* when comparing three or more nouns. Example: *The sunrise this morning was beautiful. It was more beautiful than yesterday's sunrise. It was the most beautiful sunrise this month.* Write a few multisyllable adjectives on the chalkboard and direct students to list five more at their desks. Suggestions: *wonderful, fascinating, important, ridiculous, monstrous, annoying.* Then call on sets of four students. Ask each group to name an adjective and use its different forms in three sentences.

HOW DO YOU DO IT?

Teach students that adverbs can describe verbs—they tell how something is done. Invite a student to come to the front of the class and pantomime reading a book. Ask the rest of the class to name adverbs that could describe how that student is reading. Examples: *quietly, loudly, slowly, quickly, poorly, well, passionately, expressively.* Let the student change his or her actions to match the adverbs as they are called out. Repeat the activity, pantomiming different verbs: *sleep, kick, eat, sing, paint, walk . . .*

ADJECTIVE/ADVERB PAIRS

Explain that some adjectives can be made into adverbs by adding *ly* (for example: *slow, slowly; awkward, awkwardly; happy, happily*). Point out that not all adjectives can be changed in this way. For example, *skinny* cannot become *skinnily* and *red* cannot become *redly*. Have partners work together to make two lists of words—the first with adjective-adverbs pairs and the second with adjectives that cannot be made into adverbs. Encourage students to look for words in a dictionary if they get stuck. Make your own list and challenge students to outdo your efforts.

SKETCH IT!

Like adjectives, adverbs have comparative and superlative forms.
Example: *Toto barks loudly.*
Lucky barks more loudly than Toto.
Of all the dogs, Fifi barks most loudly.
Direct students to choose an adverb. Have each student sketch and label three scenes that illustrate the adverb in its basic, comparative, and superlative forms.

fast

Kate runs fast.

Tony runs faster than Kate.

Morgan runs fastest of all.

ADD AN ADVERB

Once students understand what adverbs are, encourage them to use adverbs in their writing. Suggest that each student look over a story he or she has written and add one or two adverbs. Ask why it's probably not a good idea to add an adverb to every verb. (The story would sound overwritten.) You may want to copy passages from a chapter book you have been reading aloud to the class to model how published authors use adverbs.

PREPOSITION MYSTERY CLUES

Class Activity ......

Teach students that prepositions are words that show position or relationships between a noun (or pronoun) and another word in the sentence. Example: *Annie is under the table.* The preposition *under* shows where *Annie* is in relation to the *table.* Choose a mystery object in your classroom that is clearly visible to all students, such as the flag. Give five clues about its location that include prepositions. *It is near the . . . It is across from . . . It is over the . . .* List the prepositions on the chalkboard to reinforce the concept. Require students to ask 10 or more questions about its location that include prepositions: *Is it at the end of a stick?* Then let the class guess the answer. Choose one of your reluctant students to secretly pick the object for the next round and give five clues about it. You may want to let that student choose a partner to assist if needed.

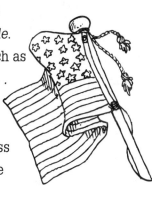

PREPOSITION POEMS

Class Activity ......

Out of the bag,
Into the pan,
Around the water,
Into the strainer,
Onto my plate,
Under the sauce,
Through my fork,
Inside my mouth,
Down to my stomach,
Spaghetti!

Read aloud this sample preposition poem. Then challenge students to write their own. Tell them to first think of a topic, such as making and eating spaghetti. Next, direct students to imagine the steps involved. Have students skip the verbs that come to mind and think of the prepositional phrase that would follow each. For example, *Take the spaghetti out of the bag* would be written as *Out of the bag.* Point out that the final line should explain or summarize the topic. After students have written the rough drafts of their poems, encourage them to see if there are any prepositions that are repeated too many times that could be replaced with other prepositions.

CONNECT IT!

Class Activity ......

Write these conjunctions on the chalkboard: *and, or, but, nor, so, for, yet.* Explain that conjunctions are words that connect words, phrases, or sentences. Ask for a student to give you a simple sentence. On the chalkboard, model how to connect that sentence to one of your own using a conjunction. Do this exercise a few times, calling on different students to supply the initial sentence and using different conjunctions to join the sentences to your own. Then call on pairs to do the same activity in front of the class without your help.

Our soccer team is really good.

Our soccer team is really good, but we still lose a lot of games.

WOW! WE DID IT! . . . OH, NO! AAAAGH!

Class Activity ......

Tell students to pretend their team just won a championship game. Give them one minute to list as many interjections as they can to match what they might say. Then have them pretend they lost the championship game. Give them another minute to list interjections that match their new feelings. Compare the lists.

The Wacky Dream

A **noun** names a person, place, or thing.
Artist, grandma, hospital, park, box, and *snake* are all nouns.

Fold the bottom of this paper so you can't see the story below.
Think of four nouns for each category—person, place, and thing.
Do not use proper nouns that need to be capitalized. Write them
on the lines. Then copy them onto the matching numbered lines
in the story. Read aloud your silly story.

Person	**Place**	**Thing**
(1)_____	(5)_____	(9)_____
(2)_____	(6)_____	(10)_____
(3)_____	(7)_____	(11)_____
(4)_____	(8)_____	(12)_____

Last night I had a wacky dream. I was walking to the (5)_____
when I saw a big (9)_____ . At first I thought it was a fake
(10)_____ . But when I got closer, I knew it was a hungry
(1)_____ . Soon I was joined by my friends. We wanted to go to the
(6)_____ to get away. But a mean (2)_____ told
us it was closed. We decided to go to the new (7)_____ instead.
It was too far to walk so we rode the (11)_____ to get there. On the
way, we saw a really scary (3)_____ . It shouted at us, "If you don't
quit staring at me, I'm going to turn you into a baby (4)_____ !"
We looked at each other and started laughing. Then a noisy
(12)_____ kept ringing. It was my alarm
clock. I was not in a crowded (8)_____ .
I was home in bed. It had all been a wacky dream.

FS123303 Grammar Made Simple Grade 4 ▪ © Frank Schaffer Publications, In

Make It a Noun

Some nouns name an idea or quality, rather than something you can see or touch. They are called **abstract nouns**. *Love, sadness, liberty,* and *imagination* are examples of abstract nouns.

Combine words in the box with suffixes in the circle to make abstract nouns. You may need to change the spelling of some words.

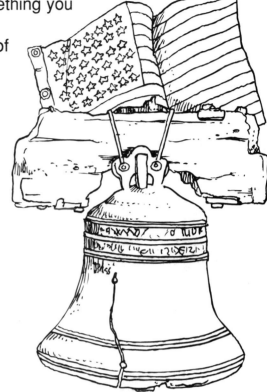

citizen	imagine
connect	inform
explore	kind
free	king
friend	pollute
friendly	punish
happy	state
ill	wise

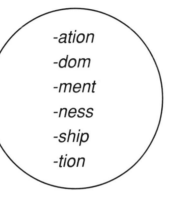

-ation
-dom
-ment
-ness
-ship
-tion

friendly   +   ness   =   friendliness

imagine   +   ation   =   imagination

1. _____ + _____ = _____

2. _____ + _____ = _____

3. _____ + _____ = _____

4. _____ + _____ = _____

5. _____ + _____ = _____

6. _____ + _____ = _____

7. _____ + _____ = _____

8. _____ + _____ = _____

9. _____ + _____ = _____

10. _____ + _____ = _____

Give It a Name

A noun that names any person, place, or thing is called a **common noun**.
A noun that names a special person, place, or thing is called a **proper noun**.
A proper noun begins with a capital letter.

Write two proper nouns for each common noun given.
Example: river—*Mississippi River, Rio Grande*

school	state	girl	boy
restaurant	author	lake	street
president	month	day	athlete
store	pet	country	planet

FS123303 Grammar Made Simple Grade 4 ▪ © Frank Schaffer Publications, In

More Than One

A **singular noun** names one person, place, thing, or idea.
A **plural noun** names more than one.

Find the plural form of each noun in the puzzle. The words will be written across or down. Circle the plural and write it beside the noun.

```
s h e e p b z w o m e n m k y
c o w c o o x e n e e o o i t
l u q h p x - r a y s u m s o
e m m i c e         a z n f s y
(a p p l e s)       r a s h e s
v i a d o g s       d q f a s v
e r r r u i z o o s u e n l a
s e t e q u e e n s a e d i s
x s i n c h e s s w i t s s e
n o e l v e s z j e l l i e s
b u s e s g r a p e s k a t y
```

apple a p p l e s

box _ _ _ _ _

child _ _ _ _ _ _ _

dog _ _ _ _ _

elf _ _ _ _ _

foot _ _ _ _

grape _ _ _ _ _ _

hand _ _ _ _ _

inch _ _ _ _ _ _

jelly _ _ _ _ _ _ _

kiss _ _ _ _ _ _

leaf _ _ _ _ _

mouse _ _ _ _

noun _ _ _ _ _

ox _ _ _ _

party _ _ _ _ _ _ _

queen _ _ _ _ _ _

rash _ _ _ _ _ _

sheep _ _ _ _ _

toy _ _ _ _

umpire _ _ _ _ _ _ _

vase _ _ _ _ _

woman _ _ _ _ _

x-ray _ - _ _ _ _

yard _ _ _ _ _

zoo _ _ _ _

Whose Shoes?

A **possessive noun** shows that a person or animal has or owns something.

baby's If it is one person or animal that has or owns something, an apostrophe **s** ('s) is added to the end.

babies' If it is more than one and already ends in an **s**, an apostrophe (') is added to the end.

children's If it is more than one but doesn't end in an **s**, an apostrophe **s** ('s) is added to the end.

Read each riddle. Write a possessive noun followed by a rhyming word for the answer. Use words from the box.

aches	brothers	pens	toys
bleachers	crayons	shoes	twigs

What do you call footwear that belongs to one gnu? ___gnu's shoes___

What do you call footwear that belong to many gnus? ___gnus' shoes___

1. What do you call games that belong to a boy? _____

   What do you call games that belong to boys? _____

2. What do you call pains that are felt by snakes? _____

   What do you call pains that are felt by a snake? _____

3. What do you call the rows of seats that belong to one teacher? _____

   What do you call the rows of seats that belong to all the teachers? _____

4. What do you call sticks that belong to three little pigs? _____

   What do you call sticks that belong to one pig? _____

5. What do you call the male siblings of one grandmother? _____

   What do you call the male siblings of two grandmothers? _____

6. What do you call *coloring* utensils that belong to the man? _____

   What do you call *writing* utensils that belong to the men? _____

Fourth **G**rade **N**ews

I, you, he, she, it, we, and *they* are all **subject pronouns**. They can take the place of a noun in the subject part of a sentence.

Read this story Max wrote for the school newspaper. Circle the subject pronouns. Write the noun each pronoun replaces.

The play _____

1. _____

2. _____

3. _____

4. _____

5. _____

6. _____

7. _____

8. _____

9. _____

10. _____

11. _____

This month Ms. Meyer's fourth-grade class put on a play. (It) was a kids' version of *Romeo and Juliet.*

The real play was written by William Shakespeare. He was a famous writer who lived about 500 years ago.

Our class did lots of work to get ready. First, Ms. Meyer read aloud books about *Romeo and Juliet* and Shakespeare. She explained the story and some of the famous lines. Then we watched a cartoon video version.

Next, our class chose parts and rehearsed. Everyone had a speaking part in the play. Most kids were in the chorus. They said rhymes that helped tell the story. Kristen Black played Juliet. She was very dramatic for a nine-year-old. Mike Schmidt played Romeo. He laughed when practicing the romantic scenes.

We also worked in groups to make scenery, props, posters, and programs. Every group had two co-leaders. They made sure the groups worked together.

Our families came to our evening performance. It went well even though a few kids forgot their lines.

Ms. Meyer proudly exclaimed, "I never thought putting on this play could be so much work, yet so much fun. You all did a wonderful job!"

Planting Bulbs

You, me, him, her, it, us, and *them* are **object pronouns**. They can take the place of a noun. They follow action verbs or prepositions, such as *to, for, of,* and *about*.

Read this story Ashley wrote.
Circle the object pronouns.
Write the noun each pronoun replaces.

Ashley and her dad

1. _____

2. _____

3. _____

4. _____

5. _____

6. _____

7. _____

8. _____

9. _____

10. _____

11. _____

12. _____

Last weekend my dad and I went to visit my grandma. She taught (us) how to plant indoor bulbs.

First, my dad had to gather a bag of rocks outside. Grandma told him that the rocks were too big, so he had to go back and get smaller ones. I had to find a shallow bowl. We filled it halfway with the pebbles.

Next, Grandma showed us the Narcissus bulbs she had bought. They looked like tiny onions. I told her I didn't think flowers would bloom from them. Grandma laughed and said, "Wait and see."

Then Grandma had me put the bulbs in the bowl with the pointy end up. I kept the bulbs in place while Grandma and my dad put more pebbles around them. The last thing we did was add water to cover the roots.

I asked Grandma when the bulbs would bloom. She told me that it would probably take four to six weeks. "Oh no, we'll miss it!" I said sadly.

"No, no," Grandma said. "This bowl is for you, Ashley!" I gave Grandma a big hug.

My dad joked, "Hey, what about me?"

"Okay," said Grandma, "they are for both of you."

FS123303 Grammar Made Simple Grade 4 ■ © Frank Schaffer Publications, I

What Does a Dog Do . . . ?

A **verb** is an action word.
Sing, draw, gallop, and *explore* are verbs.

Write four verbs to answer each question.
Do not repeat verbs.

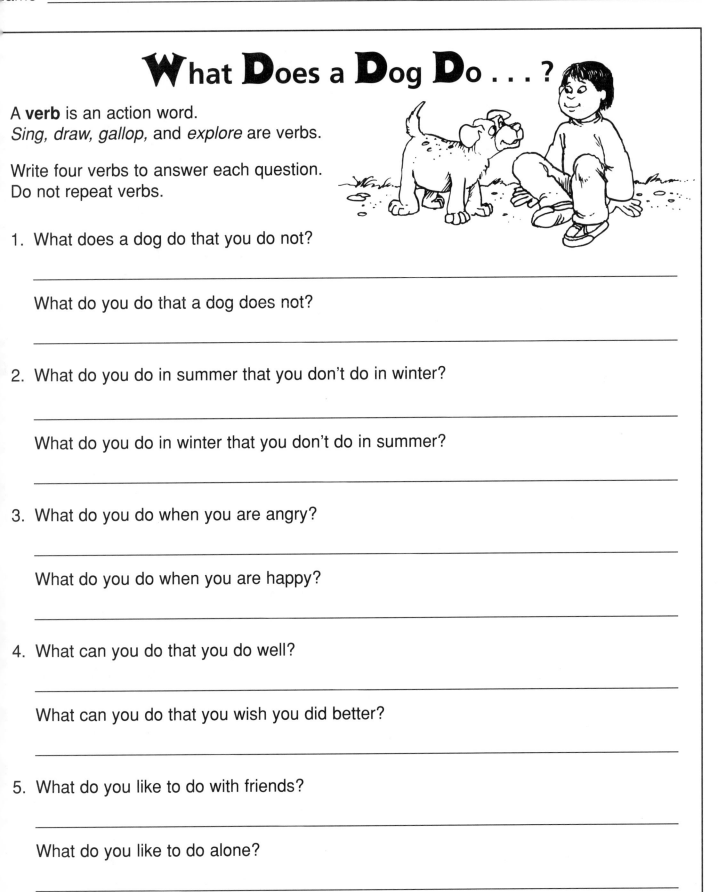

1. What does a dog do that you do not?

_____

What do you do that a dog does not?

_____

2. What do you do in summer that you don't do in winter?

_____

What do you do in winter that you don't do in summer?

_____

3. What do you do when you are angry?

_____

What do you do when you are happy?

_____

4. What can you do that you do well?

_____

What can you do that you wish you did better?

_____

5. What do you like to do with friends?

_____

What do you like to do alone?

_____

Am, Is, or Are?

Most verbs name actions. The verb **be** is different.
It tells about someone or something.
Am, is, and *are* are forms of the verb *be*.

Use **is** with one person, place, or thing.
Use **are** with more than one or with the word *you*.
Use **am** with the word *I*.

Pretend your class is at an aquarium.
Finish these statements. Use a form of the verb *be* for each.

My classmates and I <u>are excited about our field trip.</u>

1. The aquarium _____

2. I _____

3. Sea star and jellies _____

4. My teacher _____

5. You _____

6. The octopus _____

Finish these questions. Use a form of the verb *be* for each.

<u>Am</u> I <u>in the right line for the movie?</u>

7. _____ the shark tank _____

8. _____ you _____

9. _____ the sea lions _____

10. _____ we _____

11. _____ the whale skeleton _____

12. _____ I _____

FS123303 Grammar Made Simple Grade 4 ■ © Frank Schaffer Publications, Inc

Yesterday I . . .

Present tense verbs tell about actions happening now.
Past tense verbs tell about actions that happened in the past.
Most verbs are made past tense by adding *ed* to the end.

Add *ed* to make these verbs past tense. On the last line, write your own verb that fits this pattern.

paint	painted
kick	_____
gather	_____
look	_____
play	_____
answer	_____
_____	_____

Double the final consonant and add *ed* to make these verbs past tense. On the last line, write your own verb that fits this pattern.

stop	stopped
wag	_____
hum	_____
skip	_____
rub	_____
clap	_____
_____	_____

Drop the final *e* and add *ed* to make these verbs past tense. On the last line, write your own verb that fits this pattern.

skate	skated
like	_____
race	_____
smile	_____
dribble	_____
share	_____
_____	_____

Change the *y* to *i* and add *ed* to make these verbs past tense. On the last line, write your own verb that fits this pattern.

copy	copied
try	_____
multiply	_____
study	_____
hurry	_____
marry	_____

Draw, **D**rew, **D**rawn

Not all verbs are made past tense by adding *ed*.
Use this chart as a guide for **irregular past tense verbs**.

Miguel <u>draws</u> dragons very well.
He <u>drew</u> a dragon with a silver bell.
He <u>has drawn</u> its family under a spell.

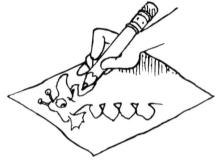

Present Tense	Past Tense	Past Participle (use with *has, had,* or *have*)	Present Tense	Past Tense	Past Participle (use with *has, had,* or *have*)
be	was, were	been	give	gave	given
begin	began	begun	go	went	gone
bite	bit	bitten	grow	grew	grown
blow	blew	blown	hide	hid	hidden
break	broke	broken	know	knew	known
bring	brought	brought	ride	rode	ridden
buy	bought	bought	see	saw	seen
choose	chose	chosen	sing	sang	sung
come	came	come	sit	sat	sat
do	did	done	speak	spoke	spoken
draw	drew	drawn	stand	stood	stood
drink	drank	drunk	swim	swam	swum
drive	drove	driven	take	took	taken
eat	ate	eaten	think	thought	thought
fall	fell	fallen	throw	threw	thrown
fly	flew	flown	wear	wore	worn
get	got	gotten	write	wrote	written

FS123303 Grammar Made Simple Grade 4 ■ © Frank Schaffer Publications, Inc

Need Some Help?

Sometimes an action verb gets help from another verb called a **helping verb**.
Here are some helping verbs: *am, is, are, was, were, been, have, has, had,
can, do, does, did, may, might, could, should, would, shall, will.*

Read these sentences. Write the verbs. Some sentences
may have a helping verb and a main verb.

__was working__   This afternoon at school I was working at the computer.

_____   1. Our class was making an animal book.

_____   2. Our teacher had assigned us different animals.

_____   3. I wrote a paragraph about lizards.

_____   4. Then I started a picture.

_____   5. I drew an entire lizard family.

_____   6. I do like lizards!

_____   7. Suddenly I saw something weird on the screen.

_____   8. A lizard tail was shaking.

_____   9. I could not believe it.

_____   10. Then its legs were moving.

_____   11. The lizard turned toward me.

_____   12. "Would you help me, please?"

_____   13. "What did you say?"

_____   14. "I am trapped on this screen."

_____   15. I called to my teacher.

_____   16. "Mrs. Furst, a lizard is talking to me!"

_____   17. She came over to my computer.

_____   18. The lizard did not move.

_____   19. "Maybe you should go to the nurse's office."

_____   20. I nodded my head.

What Is It Like?

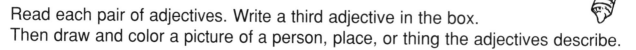

An **adjective** is a word that describes a person, place, or thing. *Yellow, hungry, five,* and *stinky* are adjectives.

Read each pair of adjectives. Write a third adjective in the box. Then draw and color a picture of a person, place, or thing the adjectives describe.

striped, alive, fast	shiny, hard,	blue, three-legged,
old, fuzzy,	round, delicious,	sad, confused,
fun, noisy,	happy, clumsy,	bumpy, wooden,

    FS123303 Grammar Made Simple Grade 4 ▪ © Frank Schaffer Publications, Inc

Smart, Smarter, Smartest

Adjectives that compare two things usually end in **er**.
Adjectives that compare three or more things usually end in **est**.
If the adjective is a long word, **more** or **most** is used with it instead.

A dog is smart.
A monkey is smarter than a dog.
A chimpanzee is probably the smartest animal of all.

Marine animals with backbones are more intelligent than those without.
A dolphin may be the most intelligent marine animal of all.

Fill in the missing adjectives in this chart. Use the last three lines to write your own examples.

Adjective	Adjective that compares two	Adjective that compares three or more
shiny	shinier	shiniest
graceful	more graceful	most graceful
	quieter	
cautious		most cautious
tall		
		brightest
beautiful		
	stronger	
		most spirited
late	later	
funny		
		nicest
	more generous	

How Does . . . ?

An **adverb** is a word that describes a verb. Some adverbs tell how something is done. They often end in *ly*. *Quickly, carefully, silently,* and *happily* are examples of adverbs.

Look at the picture. Think about how the animals are moving.
Write two adverbs for each. Do not repeat adverbs.

How does an eagle fly?
powerfully
_____

How does a bear cub climb?
_____
_____

How does a deer run?
_____
_____

How does a rabbit hop?
_____
_____

How does a turtle move?
_____
_____

How does a frog swim?
_____
_____

FS123303 Grammar Made Simple Grade 4 ▪ © Frank Schaffer Publications, Inc

Where Is It?

A **preposition** is a word that shows position between a noun and another word in a sentence. *With, from, of, at, in, out, under, next to, between,* and *over* are all prepositions. A preposition is always part of a set of words: <u>with</u> *a pen,* <u>from</u> *my house,* <u>of</u> *the family.*

Read each sentence.
Underline the prepositions.
Finish the picture to match.

Example:
The leaf fell <u>from</u> the branch, <u>near</u> the trunk, <u>onto</u> a snail.

The dog is on the rug, under the table, next to the cat.

The tennis shoes are in the closet, on the floor, between the boots and the sandals.

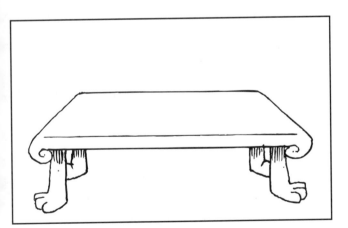

The queen is in the dining hall, at the table, with the prince.

The balloon is floating in the sky, above our heads, far from our reach.

Usage

Usage is the agreed-upon rules of language. Although various communities may have their own patterns for informal speech, it is important that students learn to speak and write standard English. Certain rules are easier to recognize and conform to, such as having nouns agree in number: *I have five sister* should be *I have five sisters.* Other rules may be more difficult or require continual practice to master.

I LIKE, HE LIKES, YOU LIKE, SHE LIKES

Class Activity

Children need to repeatedly hear language spoken correctly in order for it to become natural in their own speech and writing. Try this subject/verb agreement activity at the beginning of your language lesson. On the chalkboard, write a question that begins with the word *Who,* such as *Who likes ice cream?* Have each student in turn answer it using a different subject: *I like ice cream. Casey likes ice cream. My dog likes ice cream. . . .* If a student uses a verb that does not agree, say the sentence aloud for that child correctly. Then have the student repeat it correctly. In a few minutes, children can hear 25 correct sentences.

You can also use this lesson to teach subject/verb agreement with tricky pronouns or collective nouns. Write these or other subjects in two columns on chart paper: singular subjects—*another, anyone, each, either, everybody, everyone, everything, no one, nothing, one, other, somebody, someone, something, this, that, group, family, flock, mob*—and plural subjects—*all of them, both, few, many, most, others, several, some, these, those.* Encourage students to choose one of these subjects when answering the class question: *All of them like ice cream. Somebody likes ice cream. My family likes ice cream. . . .*

THEY ~~SEEN~~ SAW US COMING!

Class Activity

Some children (and adults) commonly misuse these past participles: *been, done, gone, known, seen.* They may use them without a needed helping verb (*has, have,* or *had*) or in place of a past tense verb. Incorrect: *They seen us coming.* Correct: *They saw us coming. They have seen us coming. They had seen us coming.* On a regular basis, write a sentence on the chalkboard that misuses a past participle. Challenge students to rewrite it correctly two different ways. Here are some starting sentences: *He been very cranky lately. Your group done us a big favor. My parents gone to the store. That bully known it was wrong. You seen that new animal show yet?*

FS123303 Grammar Made Simple Grade 4 ■ © Frank Schaffer Publications, Inc

INGULAR OR PLURAL?

a bike
an orange
one girl
five books
sixty-two million pennies
this pencil
that desk
those papers
few people

Have students work with partners. One person writes an adjective that conveys a number or amount (*a*, *an*, *one*, *five*, *sixty-two million*, *this*, *that*, *those*, *few*, *some*, *many* . . .) and the partner writes a singular or plural noun to match. Challenge pairs to write as many different sets as they can in three minutes. Then have them switch roles and repeat the activity.

ME AND . . .

earing "*Me and ___ want to . . .*" is a onstant annoyance to many a teacher nd parent. Teach students to name hemselves last. Point out that if someone ays "*Me and Mike . . . ,*" it may sound ke that person is saying *Mean Mike*. Mike is not mean! Whenever you hear a tudent name himself or herself first ("*Me nd Carla want to know if . . .*"), have the ntire class do a quick round of sentences where every student gives a different entence that follows this frame: _____ nd I _____. Soon students may notice ach other's errors with dread: "*Oh, no! ou said 'Me and Craig.' Now we'll have o . . .*"

GIVE IT TO THEM.
NO, GIVE IT TO . . .

ractice using object pronouns with this oral activity. Give students a beginning sentence that ends with an bject pronoun. Examples: *Give it to them. Would you wrap this for me? Let's write a story about you.* Call n different students to change the sentence by starting it with the word *No* and then changing the ronoun. Tell students they may include proper nouns if they are listed first and used with pronouns. xample: *Would you wrap this for me? No, would you wrap this for her? No, would you wrap this for them? No, would you wrap this for Jake and me?*

A OR AN?

Tell students that *a*, *an*, and *the* are articles—a type of adjective. Explain that *a* and *an* are used with singular nouns and *the* can be used with singular or plural nouns. Teach or review that *an* is used before words that begin with a vowel sound (*an apple, an hour*) and *a* is used before words that begin with a consonant sound (*a banana, a minute*). Let students work with partners for this activity. Tell pairs to think of related nouns (*astronaut* and *cosmonaut, ape* and *monkey, octagon* and *hexagon*) that would fit in this sentence frame: *Do you know the difference between an _____ and a _____?* Let partners alternate between asking the question and answering it. Choose whether you want pairs to do this as an oral lesson or a written one.

Do you know the difference between an opera and a musical?

No, I don't. Do you know the difference between an elf and a fairy?

GOOD OR WELL?

Teach students that *good* is an adjective. It describes a person, place, or thing. Examples: *I am a good dancer. Pizza Palace has good food.* Then explain that *well* is usually an adverb. It describes how something is done. Examples: *Rebecca dives well. My dad does not feel well today.* Divide the class into groups of four. Have each group write sentences about its members. Every student should have two sentences written about him or her—one using *good* and the other using *well*. Direct groups to underline the nouns or verbs that are being described.

THEN OR THAN?

Students often mix up *then* and *than* in their writing. Point out that *then* rhymes with *when*; it is used to signal time. *Than* is used to compare things. Have students fold a long sheet of paper into thirds. Direct them to copy and finish these sentences and to illustrate a picture to match:

Panel 1—*I used to _____ than _____.*
Panel 2—*Then _____.*
Panel 3—*Now I _____ than _____.*

I used to be 2 inches taller than my cousin.

Then he grew a lot.

Now I am shorter than he is.

I used to like math more than social studies.

Then we had Pioneer Day.

Now I like social studies more than all my other subjects.

FS123303 Grammar Made Simple Grade 4 ▪ © Frank Schaffer Publications, Inc

TONGUE TWISTERS

Homophones are words that sound alike, but have different spellings and meanings. With your class, brainstorm a list of homophones. Write the list in large letters on butcher paper to be sure students see the correct spellings. Have the student who gave a homophone pair or triplet explain the meaning of each word. Then tell students to choose a homophone set and write a tongue twister that includes all the words in the set. Examples: *Pete paints pairs and pairs of pears.*

read-red	*see-sea*	*to-too-two*
no-know	*so-sew*	*there-their-*
nose-knows	*for-four*	*they're*
you-ewe	*one-won*	*by-buy-bye*
we-wee	*eight-ate*	*rain-rein-reign*
I-eye	*ten-tin*	*new-knew-gnu*
break-brake	*braid-brayed*	*I'll-aisle-isle*
grate-great	*ball-bawl*	

TO, TOO, OR TWO?

Give each student an index card. Have them write *to* on one side of their cards and *too* on the other side. Call out a sentence that contains *to, too,* or *two.* Have students decide which word is correct and hold up that side of their cards for you to see. If the word should be *two,* tell them to hold up two fingers instead of the card. Give several sentences for practice or call on students to provide the sentences. Create and use other cards for any homophone pairs or triplets that students misuse in their writing.

NIGHT-KNIGHT

Share Harriet Ziefert's lift-the-flap book *Night Knight* (Houghton Mifflin, 1997) with your students. It features sets of homophones with one word illustrated on a flap and the other illustrated beneath it. Challenge your students to make a class lift-the-flap homophone book.

Begin by having each student pick a homophone pair that could be illustrated. Direct each student to glue one edge of a blank sheet of paper onto a larger sheet of paper. Have each student lightly trace around his or her top sheet to make a frame for the bottom sheet's picture. Next, have students write and illustrate sentences on the top flaps using one of their homophones. The illustrations should extend over the flaps at some point onto the bottom papers. Then have students lift the flaps and write and illustrate sentences within the frames using the other homophone. The illustrations should include the parts that extended off the top flaps. (In this illustration, the paint becomes part of the girl's beret.) Staple together the finished pages to make books.

My favorite color is <u>red</u>.

Last week I <u>read</u> a book.

Animal Ears

Present tense action verbs that tell about one thing have an **s** or **es** added to the end.

Present tense action verbs that tell about more than one thing or follow the pronouns *you* or *I* do not have an **s** or **es** added to the end.

An elephant uses its big ears to cool off.
I use my big ears to hear!

Write the correct verb.

1. An elephant _____ low sounds, called infrasound,

   that humans cannot hear. (make, makes)

2. Other elephants _____ the sounds from far away. (hear, hears)

3. In this way, elephants _____ each other if danger is near. (warn, warns)

4. Bats _____ sounds we can't hear either. (make, makes)

5. A bat _____ high sounds, called ultrasound. (emit, emits)

6. The sound waves _____ off objects

   and help the bat find its way. (bounce, bounces)

7. Dolphins also _____ sound waves to find their ways. (use, uses)

8. They _____ clicking sounds that echo through water. (make, makes)

9. A dolphin _____ for the echoes with its ears and jaw. (listen, listens)

10. Male crickets _____ to attract female crickets. (sing, sings)

11. A female cricket _____ the song

    using ears found on her front legs. (hear, hears)

12. Owls _____ at night. (hunt, hunts)

13. Their excellent hearing _____ them find prey. (help, helps)

14. An owl _____ the sound

    of a mouse hundreds of yards away. (hear, hears)

 FS123303 Grammar Made Simple Grade 4 ▪ © Frank Schaffer Publications, Inc

Meet Zippisplat

Zippisplat is an alien. She landed on Earth in the United States. She is learning to speak English. Zippisplat needs help using forms of the verb **be—am, is,** and **are**.

Read Zippisplat's introduction. Underline the word **be** whenever you find it. Rewrite the paragraphs using the correct verbs.

Use **is** with one person, place, or thing.
Use **are** with more than one or with the word *you*.
Use **am** with the word *I*.
Use **be** after the word *to*.

My name be Zippisplat. I be an alien. I come from the planet Splat. It be far, far away from Earth. Splat be a wonderful planet.

I be visiting Earth for one month. My family be not here with me. They be still on Splat. I miss them very much. I even miss my little brother. He be sometimes a brat, but I love him.

I be happy to be here because Earthlings be very friendly.

_____
_____
_____
_____
_____
_____
_____
_____
_____

Travel the World

Read this story Patrice wrote.
Circle the **verbs** that are incorrect.
Write the correct verb on the line.

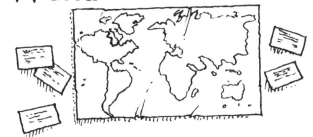

made

1. _____
2. _____
3. _____
4. _____
5. _____
6. _____
7. _____
8. _____
9. _____
10. _____
11. _____
12. _____
13. _____
14. _____
15. _____

Last week my friends and I (make) a geography game called "Travel the World." It were for a social studies project at school.

First we finded a large map of the world. Our map showed each of the continents in a different color.

Then we thinked of game ideas. I told our group about a game I seen at the store once. Megan had the best idea. She say the purpose of the game should be to visit every continent. We choosed her idea.

Ben and I writed cards for the game. The cards told the players which continent to go to. For example, one card sayed this: *Go to the continent where the Nile River is found.* Theo thought our cards might be too hard for some kids. So we add the name of the continent on each card also. Megan and Theo maked score sheets. The score sheets haved check-off boxes next to each continent name.

We played the game to test it. I keeped picking cards that sent me to South America or Europe. I never did get a card for Asia. Ben winned our practice game.

Finally we turn in our project. Our teacher liked it. He letted us teach the class how to play it that day.

FS123303 Grammar Made Simple Grade 4 ▪ © Frank Schaffer Publications, Inc.

Neighborhood Bake Sale

Read these sentences Elise wrote.
Decide if the missing word should be a **singular noun** or **plural noun**.
Write the correct noun on the line.

Our favorite neighbors live across the ___street___ from us. (street, streets)

1. There are three _____ in their family—Sara, Ilana, and Lucas. (kid, kids)

2. Last Saturday Sara suggested we bake a _____. (dessert, desserts)

3. Ilana and I looked in cookbooks for _____ . (recipe, recipes)

4. The dessert _____ all looked great. (picture, pictures)

5. We decided to bake an apple _____ . (pie, pies)

6. Ilana thought we should make up our own _____ for it. (recipe, recipes)

7. Lucas and my little sister Katherine gathered

   _____ for us. (ingredient, ingredients)

8. We told them to get flour, salt, sugar, shortening, water,

   cinnamon, and some _____. (apple, apples)

9. The apples were easy to find because our

   apple _____ are full of them now. (tree, trees)

10. We mixed the dough for a pie _____ . (crust, crusts)

11. Katherine and Lucas wanted to make _____ too. (cookie, cookies)

12. They took some of our dough and mixed in one _____. (egg, eggs)

13. They rolled the dough into _____ and sprinkled sugar on them. (ball, balls)

14. Our _____ smelled so good we decided to sell them. (dessert, desserts)

15. We made a big bake sale _____ and took turns holding it. (sign, signs)

16. About ten _____ who drove down our street

    stopped and bought things. (person, people)

17. We ate all the _____! (leftover, leftovers)

Be Polite

When you speak or write about someone else
and yourself, name yourself last.
Use **I** when you are part of the subject.
Use **me** when the subject is doing something to or with you.

Elizabeth and I are building a model rocket.
Ethan wants to help Elizabeth and me launch it.

For each sentence below, write the name of a classmate and either the pronoun **me** or **I**.

 My classmates and ___I___ are studying space.

1. Our teacher chose _____ and _____

   for a demonstration of how the Moon revolves around the Earth.

2. Then _____ and _____ acted out how the Earth revolves around

   the Sun.

3. My best friend lent _____ and _____

   a calculator for solving math problems.

4. _____ and_____ like to figure out

   how much we would weigh on different planets.

5. The principal gave _____ and _____

   an award for our space shuttle report.

6. _____ and_____ invited an astronaut to come to our class.

7. She showed _____ and _____ pictures from her spaceflight.

8. In art class, _____ and _____

   are working on a mobile of the solar system.

9. Last year _____ and _____ made a giant model of Jupiter.

10. The librarian helped _____ and _____ find a book of star myths.

11. _____ and _____ want to write our own myth.

12. In my story, a kindergartner turns _____ and _____ into stars.

A Fun Book

Read the story. Fill in the missing pronouns.

Subject Pronoun	Object Pronoun
I	me
he	him
she	her
it	it
we	us
you	you
they	them

One of my favorite books is *Free Stuff for Kids.** My aunt gave it to _____ for my birthday. _____ told me my cousins have the book and like _____ a lot. The book has all kinds of things you can send away for. Some of _____ are free and others cost a dollar or less.

I sent away for a free sticker from the Detroit Tigers. First _____ wrote a letter asking for the Tigers' fan pack. I had to write _____ very neatly. The book instructed me to include a self-addressed, stamped envelope. If you don't remember the envelope, the place might not send _____ your stuff. I mailed my letter and waited. Then _____ waited some more.

One day my dad said I got a letter. I asked _____ who sent it. He said the Detroit Tigers. I quickly opened _____ up. The Tigers sent _____ more than a sticker. _____ gave me a schedule, roster, fact sheet, and photo, too.

The next letter _____ wrote was to my aunt. I thanked _____ for my book.

Now I am going to look through the book with my best friend. _____ will pick out some new stuff together to send away for.

Free Stuff for Kids (Simon and Schuster, 1998)

A Clarinet and An Oboe

A and **an** are special adjectives called **articles**.
They are used to describe a singular noun (one person, place, or thing).

Choose **a** or **an** to write before each instrument on this list.
Use **a** if the next word begins with a consonant sound.
Use **an** if the next word begins with a vowel sound.
Look out for 24—it's tricky!

_a_____ clarinet

_an_____ oboe

1. _____ alto saxophone
2. _____ tenor saxophone
3. _____ flute
4. _____ piccolo
5. _____ algaita
6. _____ bassoon
7. _____ ocarina
8. _____ French horn
9. _____ English horn
10. _____ Alphorn
11. _____ trumpet
12. _____ didjeridu
13. _____ trombone
14. _____ tuba
15. _____ accordion
16. _____ electric piano
17. _____ grand piano
18. _____ organ

19. _____ bass guitar
20. _____ electric guitar
21. _____ acoustic guitar
22. _____ cello
23. _____ violin
24. _____ ukelele
25. _____ harp
26. _____ Irish harp
27. _____ Veracruz harp
28. _____ sitar
29. _____ 'ud
30. _____ zither
31. _____ Appalachian dulcimer
32. _____ bass drum
33. _____ steel drum
34. _____ odaiko
35. _____ xylophone
36. _____ gong ageng
37. _____ glockenspiel
38. _____ harmonica

FS123303 Grammar Made Simple Grade 4 ▪ © Frank Schaffer Publications, Inc

Bear Facts

Read each sentence.
Fill in the circle next to the correct adjective. Use the chart as a guide.

Adjective	Adjective that compares two	Adjective that compares three or more
strong	stronger	strongest
powerful	more powerful	most powerful
good	better	best

1. A black bear is ___. It can run 25 miles per hour.
   - ○ fast
   - ○ faster

2. A polar bear is ___ than a black bear.
   - ○ fast
   - ○ faster

3. A brown bear may be the ___ of all bears.
   - ○ faster
   - ○ fastest

4. A sloth bear is very ___. Its name even means *slow*.
   - ○ slow
   - ○ slower

5. All large bears are ___ swimmers.
   - ○ good
   - ○ best

6. But polar bears are the ___ swimmers of all.
   - ○ good
   - ○ best

7. A male bear is usually ____ than a female.
   - ○ larger
   - ○ largest

8. The ____ bear ever found was a polar bear.
   - ○ larger
   - ○ largest

9. That ____ bear weighed more than 2,000 pounds.
   - ○ huge
   - ○ hugest

10. A bear cub is quite ____ when it is born.
    - ○ tiny
    - ○ tinier

11. It is ____ than a human baby.
    - ○ tiny
    - ○ tinier

12. A mother bear is very ____.
    - ○ protective
    - ○ more protective

13. A female bear with cubs is ____ than a male bear.
    - ○ ferociouser
    - ○ more ferocious

14. Grizzly cubs are ____ climbers than their moms.
    - ○ gooder
    - ○ better

15. Adult grizzlies are too ____ to climb trees.
    - ○ heavy
    - ○ heavier

It's Quite a Cat!

Read each sentence.
Write the correct missing word.
When you choose a contraction,
check if it is correct by reading
aloud the two words it stands for.

Contraction		Possessive
it's	(it is)	its (belongs to it)
you're	(you are)	your (belongs to you)
they're	(they are)	their (belongs to them)

Have you met __your__ new neighbors? (your, you're)

1. _____ cat is strange. (Their, They're)

2. I think it is chasing _____ dog Rufus. (your, you're)

3. _____ the wildest cat I have ever seen. (Its, It's)

4. _____ going to have to protect Rufus. (Your, You're)

5. It looks like _____ neighbors are going out. (your, you're)

6. _____ leaving the cat in the yard. (Their, They're)

7. Let's try to trick _____ cat. (their, they're)

8. We'll bark like Rufus to get _____ attention. (its, it's)

9. _____ coming now–keep barking. (Its, It's)

10. Oh, no! _____ in trouble. (Your, You're)

11. The cat is bringing something from _____ yard. (their, they're)

12. I think _____ carrying one of Rufus's old bones. (its, it's)

13. Aaaagh! That cat is going to bonk _____ head with the bone. (your, you're)

14. _____ okay, aren't you? (Your, You're)

15. Let's go tell _____ parents what happened. (your, you're)

16. _____ not going to believe this story. (Their, They're)

17. _____ good enough to be in the newspaper. (Its, It's)

18. The headline will read: *Cat Gets* _____ *Revenge—*

    Attacks Foolish Kids With Dog Bone. (Its, It's)

FS123303 Grammar Made Simple Grade 4 ▪ © Frank Schaffer Publications, In

Knew York or New York?

Homophones are words that sound alike but have different spellings and meanings.

Fill in the circle next to the correct homophone for each sentence.

1. My family is planning a trip to ____ York State.
   - ○ Knew
   - ○ New

2. We each get to pick ____ place to visit.
   - ○ one
   - ○ won

3. My mom ____ to go see the Statue of Liberty.
   - ○ once
   - ○ wants

4. It stands ____ New York Harbor.
   - ○ in
   - ○ inn

5. My dad wants ____ visit the Guggenheim Museum.
   - ○ to
   - ○ two

6. ____ a famous building designed by Frank Lloyd Wright.
   - ○ Its
   - ○ It's

7. Of course, the museum has lots of great art, ____.
   - ○ to
   - ○ too

8. My sister has ____ books about Harriet Tubman.
   - ○ read
   - ○ red

9. She wants to go ____ Harriet Tubman's home in Auburn.
   - ○ sea
   - ○ see

10. And me, ____ do I want to go?
    - ○ wear
    - ○ where

11. I thought it over ____ a long time.
    - ○ for
    - ○ four

12. I ____ like to see Niagara Falls.
    - ○ wood
    - ○ would

13. It is on the ____ between New York and Canada.
    - ○ boarder
    - ○ border

14. I ____ this will be a wonderful vacation.
    - ○ know
    - ○ no

Mechanics

Oral language does not involve mechanics, but written language does. Mechanics includes the rules for capitalization and punctuation that help a reader decipher writing. The more students read and write, the greater their needs and the greater their opportunities for learning the mechanics of English.

WRITE THE RULES

Group Activity

Begin a study of capitalization by evaluating what students already know. Divide the class into groups of four. Challenge each group to write a list of rules that explain when words need to be capitalized. Elicit an example from the class and model how you want the rule to be written. Direct students to make the rules specific. For example, rather than writing *All proper nouns must be capitalized*, students should write several rules and give examples: *Names and titles of people need to be capitalized (Rachel Carson, Dr. Mason, General Washington). Names of landforms and bodies of water need to be capitalized (Mount St. Helens, Connecticut River, Lake Superior).* Give groups about 30 minutes to complete the activity. Then collect and analyze their rules to determine what your class knows and needs to learn.

ANASTASIA'S LISTS

Class Activity

In Lois Lowry's novel *Anastasia Krupnik* (Dell Publishing, 1979), each chapter ends with 10-year-old Anastasia's current lists of Things I Love and Things I Hate. Invite students to make their own lists. Direct them to capitalize the headings and any proper nouns on their lists. Explain that common nouns should be written with lowercase letters. You may want to do a sample list to model the activity for students.

Things I Love	Things I Hate
my family	homework
Disneyland	cleaning my room
putting on plays	my brother Alex
pizza	(sometimes)
Taco Bell	
my brother Alex (sometimes)	

Homework

Where Were You Born?

Give students practice capitalizing proper nouns with this family-centered homework activity. Direct students to find out where five people in their families were born (siblings, parents, aunts, uncles, cousins, or grandparents). Have them write a complete sentence for each person that includes one or more proper nouns (city, state, country, hospital, or address). Examples: *I was born at Torrance Community Hospital in Torrance, California. My sister was born at home in San Pedro, California. My great-grandparents on my dad's side were born in Warsaw, Poland.* You can use the homework papers later to teach or review the use of commas between a city and state or city and country.

FS123303 Grammar Made Simple Grade 4 ▪ © Frank Schaffer Publications, I

BOOK TITLES

Group Activity

Divide the class into groups of four. Direct groups to analyze the covers of 10 or more books to figure out which words in a title are capitalized. After about five minutes, let groups share their findings. You may want to ask questions to guide students' thinking. Example: *Does anyone have a book title where the word the begins with a capital letter? Does anyone have a title where the is not capitalized? Where is the word the in each title?* Summarize or supplement your students' findings with these rules:

1. The first word and last word in a title are always capitalized.

2. Articles (*a, an, the*), short conjunctions (*and*), and short prepositions (*in, of, to, for . . .*) in the middle of a title are not capitalized.

3. All other words are capitalized.

Then give students practice writing book titles. Challenge each group to make up and write titles for these or other categories: a funny book, a scary book, an animal book, a craft book, a really boring book . . .

UNDERLINE OR *ITALICS*

Class Activity

Teach students that when they are handwriting a sentence that contains a book title, the title is underlined. Then explain that if they type the sentence on a computer, the title can be underlined or written in italics. Do a computer lesson for a follow-up. Have students type and complete this paragraph:

> When I was in kindergarten, my favorite book was _____. This year my favorite book is _____. A book I would like to read in the future is _____.

Direct students to use the underlining tool for their book titles. Next, have them copy the paragraph and paste it below the original one. Teach students how to highlight and change the underlined title to italics. Reinforce that a book title should be underlined or italicized, but not both.

DEAR SECRET PAL

Class Activity

Teach students the correct form for a friendly letter. (See page 4 for a guideline.) Point out that the first word of the greeting and closing are capitalized. Then have each student write a Secret Pal letter. The body of each letter should be a paragraph with clues about its mystery author. The letter should also include the date, a greeting, a closing, and a question mark for the signature. Collect the letters and distribute them on a different day. Tell students to read their letters and to write a guess about its author at the bottom. Post the letters on a bulletin board. Let students find their own letters and sign their names at the bottom.

> *October 8, 2002*
>
> *Dear Secret Pal,*
>
> *I like science, geography, and music. My favorite things to read are joke books and maps. I like to swim and play kickball. I also like to make candles. I have two pets. Can you guess who I am?*
>
> *Your mystery pal,*
> *?*
>
> **I think this mystery person is Neal.**
>
> *No, I am the mystery pal! Sonia*

ABBREVIATIONS POSTER

Class Activity

Ask the class to name abbreviations they know. List them on the chalkboard and next to them write the words they represent. Use the examples to teach or review these guidelines:

1. Words that begin with a capital letter are capitalized when they are abbreviated.

2. Most abbreviations have a period at the end.

3. Postal abbreviations for states are two capital letters with no period.

Give each student a large piece of tagboard. Tell students they have one week to find, cut out, and glue to their tagboards as many abbreviations as possible. Brainstorm a list of sources: mail, newspaper, food packaging, catalogs, and so on. When students have completed the assignment, discuss which abbreviations are most common and which, if any, students might not know.

AVENUE—AVE.

Class Activity

Play this game at the chalkboard. Divide the class into four teams and assign each its own chalkboard section. Call out a word, such as *Avenue*. Have the first player on each team write it. Help them with spelling as needed. Then have those players write the abbreviation. Teams earn one point for each correct answer. Team members who are not at the board may not speak, but may write and hold up clues. Continue playing until all students have had several turns.

SILENT CONVERSATION

Partner Activity

Direct students to work with partners and hold silent conversations. Write this question frame on the chalkboard and have one student in each pair copy and finish it to begin the conversation: *What is your favorite _____?* No talking is permitted. Instead, partners should write questions and answers back and forth to each other. Tell students that the conversations must be written in the form of complete sentences that begin with a capital letter and end with the correct punctuation mark (. or ? or !).

WHAT DID THEY SAY?

Class Activity

Invite two volunteers to come to the front of the class. Ask them to hold a brief conversation—each person says one or two lines twice. While they are speaking, write their conversation on the chalkboard using running text (no indentation or quotation marks). Then tell the volunteers to return to their seats. Have the class compare hearing a conversation with reading one. Ask them what writers do to make a conversation clearer to readers. Here are some ideas to bring out in the discussion:

1. The speaker's exact words are enclosed in quotation marks.

2. Phrases are added before, after, or between those words to clarify the speaker (*said Kevin, Gina shouted*).

3. A new paragraph is started each time the speaker changes.

FS123303 Grammar Made Simple Grade 4 ▪ © Frank Schaffer Publications, In

"CAN YOU FIND A QUESTION IN A BOOK?" SHE ASKED.

Punctuating dialogue may be the most difficult area of mechanics that your students encounter. To avoid overwhelming your students, choose one type of sentence and focus on how it is punctuated. For example, begin with dialogue that involves questions. (Save declarative sentences for last.) Challenge students to hunt through picture books or chapter books for lines of dialogue that include questions. Tell them to copy five examples they find. Elicit sample sentences from your students and write them on the chalkboard. Analyze how the sentences are punctuated. (*Quotation marks surround the exact words a speaker says. The question mark goes inside the quotation marks. If the phrase identifying the speaker comes before the exact words spoken, it is followed by a comma. If the phrase identifying the speaker comes after the exact words spoken, it ends with a period.*) Then have students write their own sample dialogues made of questions. Using these steps, teach each type of sentence at a slow pace.

DEAR LEONARDO

Brainstorm what children already know about writing a friendly letter. Teach or review how commas are used in three places: between the day and year in the date, at the end of the greeting, and at the end of the closing. Then have students work with partners and write fan letters to people they admire. Each student should write his or her own letter, but pairs can talk to each other for ideas. When partners finish, they should help each other proofread the letters. Write a proofreading checklist for students on the chalkboard. On another day, have partners exchange letters and pretend to be the admired people receiving the letters. Tell students to write friendly reply letters. Once again, have pairs proofread their work. Post the completed sets on a bulletin board.

ENVELOPE TIME

Teach students how to address an envelope. Point out that the information needs to be written neatly and correctly or the postal service may not be able to deliver the letter. Sketch a huge envelope on butcher paper. Model for students where and how to write the name and address of the person to whom the letter is being sent. Next, show where and how to write the sender's name and address. Ask students which letters or words are capitalized and how the envelope is punctuated. Have students address envelopes to their parents, using the school address for the return address. Inside the envelopes, have students place a class newsletter or a friendly letter they have written detailing what they are learning. Mail the letters. For additional letter–writing information and activities, read aloud Loreen Leedy's informative and friendly book *Messages in the Mailbox* (Holiday, 1991).

JIMMY JOE AND JASMINE

Write this sentence on the chalkboard: *Jimmy Joe and Jasmine went to the office.* Ask students how many kids went to the office—two or three? State that, according to the way the sentence was written, two children went—Jasmine and Jimmy Joe. Explain that when there are three or more items in a series, a comma is used to make the sentence clearer. Therefore, if the author meant that three kids went, the sentence should look like this: *Jimmy, Joe, and Jasmine went to the office.* Tell students to write sentences, based on what they observe in the classroom, that involve three items in a series. Model a few examples to get students started.

> *Sean is wearing a black shirt, black jeans, and black tennis shoes.*
>
> *Angela, Brian, and Felicia are working together in a group.*
>
> *Ms. Blakemore is sitting at her desk, holding a pencil, and staring out the window.*

CONTRACTION EQUATIONS

> *Who + _____ = Who'll*
>
> *should + not = _____*

Use an addition equation format to review with students how contractions are formed: *did + not = didn't.* Explain as needed how the apostrophe takes the place of the omitted letters. Then have pairs of students work together to write 20 contraction equations. Tell them to leave blanks for either one of the addends (words) or the sum (contraction). You may want to write on the chalkboard words that are commonly found in contractions: *I, you, he, she, it, we, they, who, what, there, that, am, is, are, have, has, had, will, do, does, did, could, should, would, not.*

WHOSE?

Teach students that possessive nouns answer the question *Whose?* Example: *Maria's skirt/Whose skirt? Maria's.* Give students 10 small self-sticking notes. Have them write *Whose?* on each. Next, direct students to skim through books looking for apostrophes that might signal possessive nouns. Tell students to ask themselves, *Is it a contraction made of two words or a possessive noun that answers the question "Whose?"* If it is a possessive noun, have them stick one of their notes above the noun that tells what is being possessed. Direct students to continue until they have placed all 10 notes. Finish by letting each student share one of his or her examples with the class. Later, when you encounter missing apostrophes for possessive nouns in students' work, stick on a note that simply says *Whose?* Students should know to add the missing apostrophe.

A SUPER SCHEDULE

Colons are used most commonly by fourth–grade students when writing time. Have each student write a schedule for an ideal day at school. Direct them to include at least six different times in their schedules. Point out that a colon is used to separate the hours from minutes. You may also want students to use the abbreviations *a.m.* or *p.m.* to indicate morning or afternoon.

Places to Visit

A **proper noun** names a particular person, place, or thing. It begins with a capital letter.

Read the paragraph. There are 16 words that should be capitalized that are not. Underline three times each letter that should be a capital. The first one is done for you.

Last summer my family took a trip to yellowstone national Park. The huge park is in three states— wyoming, montana, and idaho. We camped at grant Village beside yellowstone lake. My brother, michael, and I had our own tent. On the first day, we went to see old Faithful. Old faithful is a geyser that shoots up water about once an hour. Another day we went horseback riding near roosevelt lodge. President teddy roosevelt used to ride horses at the park. We had lots of fun on our trip. I want to go back to yellowstone.

Write a paragraph about a place you like to visit. Be sure to capitalize any proper nouns.

_____

_____

_____

_____

_____

_____

_____

_____

_____

Dear **D**r. **D**oolittle

In a friendly letter, these words begin with a capital letter:

- the date
- the first word in the greeting and the closing
- the first word in each sentence
- the names of particular people, places, or things
- the pronoun "I"

Date	May 1, 2003
Greeting	Dear Dr. Doolittle,
Body	I have a terrible toothache. My friend Cheerful Chipmunk told me you help animals. Could I come see you this Thursday?
Closing	Yours truly,
Signature	Busy Beaver

Read this letter. There are 15 words that need to be capitalized. Underline three times each letter that should be a capital.

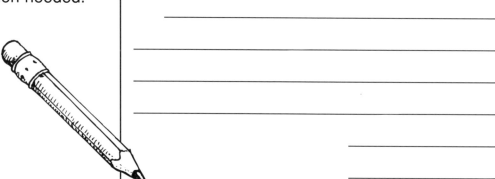

may 2, 2003

dear busy beaver,

   i would be happy to help you. please do not wait until thursday. come as soon as you can. my address is 123 w. animal drive.

      your friend,

      dr. doolittle

Write a thank-you note from Busy Beaver to Dr. Doolittle. Be sure to use capital letters when needed.

_____

_____,

_____

_____

_____

_____,

_____

Make It Shorter

An **abbreviation** is a shorter way of writing a word or group of words.
An abbreviation usually has a period (.) at the end of it.
If the word begins with a capital letter, its abbreviation should also.

Draw lines to match each word to its abbreviation.

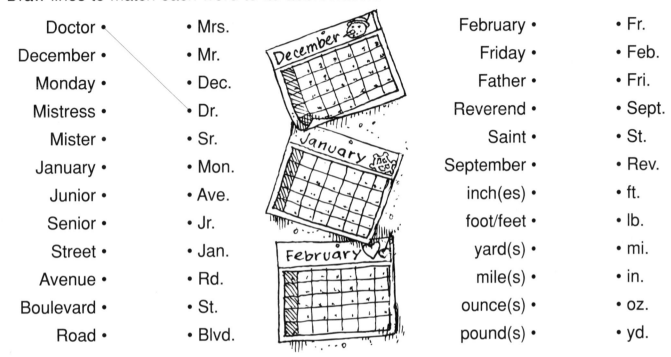

Doctor •	• Mrs.
December •	• Mr.
Monday •	• Dec.
Mistress •	• Dr.
Mister •	• Sr.
January •	• Mon.
Junior •	• Ave.
Senior •	• Jr.
Street •	• Jan.
Avenue •	• Rd.
Boulevard •	• St.
Road •	• Blvd.

February •	• Fr.
Friday •	• Feb.
Father •	• Fri.
Reverend •	• Sept.
Saint •	• St.
September •	• Rev.
inch(es) •	• ft.
foot/feet •	• lb.
yard(s) •	• mi.
mile(s) •	• in.
ounce(s) •	• oz.
pound(s) •	• yd.

Rewrite these names or phrases using abbreviations for one of the words.

1. Martin Luther King, Junior _____

2. Saint Louis, Missouri _____

3. Peña Boulevard _____

4. Doctor McCandless _____

5. State Street _____

6. Mister Thomas A. Edison _____

7. February 14th _____

8. Pennsylvania Avenue _____

9. Mistress Eleanor Roosevelt _____

10. 7 pounds _____

Add the **M**arks

Read this story Dennis wrote. Add the missing **punctuation marks**.
Write a period (**.**) at the end of statements.
Write a question mark (**?**) at the end of questions.
Write an exclamation mark (**!**) at the end of sentences that show
strong feeling.

Have you ever had a really bad day   Yesterday was the

worst day of my life   I made a fool of myself at my piano recital

I like taking piano lessons   My piano teacher is friendly and

helpful   Twice a year we have a piano recital   Each student plays a song he or she

knows well

A month ago my piano teacher had asked, "What song do you want to play, Dennis   "

"Could I play *Für Elise*   " I asked.

"Certainly   " she exclaimed. "That would be a great piece for you   "

Für Elise is a song by Beethoven   I practiced it over and over again

I could play it perfectly at home

My parents and my grandparents came to my recital   When I saw my granddad, I

started to get nervous   He plays the piano in a jazz band   What would he think of me

When it was my turn to play, I looked out at the audience   What a crowd   Instead of

playing like I do at home, I played slowly and softly   I hit a wrong note and then another

Finally it was over   I stood up to take my bow and turned bright red

After the recital, we went out for dessert   My granddad

could tell I was in a bad mood   "What's wrong   " he asked.

"I played horribly   "

He said, "Every musician has a bad day now and then   "

"What do you do when you get nervous, Granddad   " I asked him.

"I pretend I'm home alone with no audience," he answered. "Try it next time   "

   FS123303 Grammar Made Simple Grade 4 ▪ © Frank Schaffer Publications, In

Yo-Yo Time

Use **quotation marks** (" ") to show the exact words a speaker says.
"Class," said our gym teacher, "I'd like you to meet yo-yo champion Yolanda Post."
Yolanda asked, "What tricks would you like to learn?"
"I want to learn how to make a yo-yo sleep," Kyle replied.

Read the conversation below. Add the missing quotation marks.
Continue the conversation by writing the words of three more speakers.

We get to do yo-yos in gym today,
announced Rebecca.

Did you bring a yo-yo?   asked Jake.

Yes, I brought the new one I got for my
birthday,   answered Rebecca.

Nathan chimed in,   I don't have one.

Don't worry,   said Rebecca,   Ms. James
has yo-yos for everybody.

Nathan asked,   Do you know any tricks?

I can do Walk the Dog,   said Jake.   Watch!

Wow! That's cool!   exclaimed Nathan and Rebecca.

I am learning Rock the Baby,   said Rebecca.   I'll show you.

That was pretty good,   said Nathan.

I can do it better,   said Rebecca.   Let me try it again.

Hey, you did it!   shouted Jake.   That was great.

_____

_____

_____

_____

_____

"**W**atch **O**ut, **R**ed!"

Use **quotation marks** (" ") to show the exact words a speaker says.
"Grandmother, what big eyes you have!" exclaimed Red Riding Hood.
The Wolf replied sweetly, "The better to see you with, my dear."

Use a **comma** (,) to set off the exact words a speaker says from the rest of the sentence.
"Grandmother," said Red Riding Hood, "you don't look so good."
"I'm fine," said the Wolf.
Red Riding Hood continued, "Your ears look a little swollen."

If a speaker's exact words need a **question mark** (?) or **exclamation mark** (!), write the mark inside the quotation marks.
Red Riding Hood asked, "Grandmother, was your nose always that big?"
"Don't be rude, young lady!" snapped the Wolf. "My nose is swollen from this illness."

Read the conversation below.
Add quotation marks and missing punctuation to the characters' lines.

I brought you this basket of goodies said Red Riding Hood.

Your hand, er, I mean the basket, looks quite tasty   replied the Wolf.   Thank you, dear.

Red Riding Hood asked   Grandmother, would you like me to read you a story
That would be lovely   said the Wolf.
I'll sit here in this rocking chair   said Red Riding Hood.
Please come sit on my bed, dear,   pleaded the Wolf   so I may hear you better.
With those big ears, you could hear me at my home   mumbled Red Riding Hood.
Watch it, smart aleck   exclaimed the Wolf, grabbing Red Riding Hood.
Let me go   shouted Red Riding Hood.
The only place you are going is inside me   said the Wolf cruelly.
Red Riding Hood quickly squirmed out of the Wolf's grasp and asked   Where is my grandmother

   FS123303 Grammar Made Simple Grade 4 ■ © Frank Schaffer Publications, Inc

Commas in **H**istory

Use a **comma** (,) to separate a city from a state or country.
We are going to visit San Antonio, Texas.
My family has relatives in Monterrey, Mexico.

Use a **comma** (,) to separate the month and day from the year.
The Declaration of Independence was adopted on July 4, 1776.

Read these sentences. Add the missing commas.

1. Christopher Columbus landed in the West Indies on October 12 1492.

2. The largest metropolitan area in North America is Mexico City Mexico.

3. Many people speak French in Montreal Canada.

4. You may see bull sharks in Lake Nicaragua if you visit Granada Nicaragua.

5. Delaware became the first state to ratify the U.S. Constitution on December 7 1787.

6. Hawaii became the 50th U.S. state on August 21 1959.

7. The highest North American temperature was 134°F at Death Valley California.

8. The lowest North American temperature was -87°F at Northice Greenland.

9. Several Central American countries declared their independence from Spain on
   September 15 1821.

10. The Mississippi River flows into the Gulf of Mexico near New Orleans Louisiana.

11. The Battle of the Little Bighorn, or "Custer's Last Stand," was fought on
    June 25 1876.

12. The sun never sets from May 10 to August 2 at Point Barrow Alaska.

13. On December 17 1903, the Wright Brothers flew the first powered airplane.

14. Canada's official flag flew for the first time on February
    15 1965.

15. The world's busiest airport is in Chicago Illinois.

16. Many tourists visit beautiful Montego Bay Jamaica.

Dear Ms. Spider

In a friendly letter, use a **comma** (,) in these places:

- between the day and year in the date
- at the end of the greeting
- at the end of the closing

Date	July 28, 2004
Greeting	Dear Mr. Fly,
Body	I am having a tea party at my web this Monday. Would you please come?
Closing	Yours truly,
Signature	Ms. Spider

Read this letter.
Write the missing commas.

July 29 2004

Dear Ms. Spider

    Thank you for your invitation. I do try to avoid spider webs. Could we meet somewhere else? Please let me know.

    Your acquaintance

    Mr. Fly

Write Ms. Spider's reply. Follow the examples to indent your letter correctly.

Silly Riddles

A **comma** (,) tells the reader to pause.

Use a comma to separate the person being spoken to from what is being said.
Ladies and gentlemen, our show is about to begin.
Do you know what Miss Anthony's class is doing for the talent show, Nicole?

Use a comma after *Yes, No,* or an interjection at the beginning of a sentence.
Yes, they are telling riddles.
No, Dillon, I don't know.
Wow, did you see that?

Read each set of sentences. Add the missing commas.

1. Adam what did the mayonnaise say to the refrigerator?
   I don't know Bonnie what?
   Close the door, I'm dressing!

2. Larry where do cows go for fun?
   To a playground?
   No to the moo-vies!

3. Jessica where do sheep get their hair cut?
   I don't know Daniel. At a hair salon?
   At the baa-baa shop!
   Ugh I should have known that!

4. Bobby what animals like to write letters?
   Snakes?
   No pigs.
   I don't get it Kim.
   They're pen pals!

5. Melanie do you know any riddles?
   Yes I do Miss Anthony. What is black and white and red all over?
   A newspaper?
   No an embarrassed zebra!

Asia, Africa, and Australia

A **comma** (,) tells the reader to pause.

Use a comma to separate words in a series of three or more items.
Scott sings scales to scarecrows, sketches skunks, and scouts for squirrels.
Doug, Diana, Daphne, and Damon dine on delicious desserts.

Read each sentence. Add the missing commas.

1. Otis ordered oysters oranges olives or oatmeal.

2. Will Wanda wait for William Winston and Winifred?

3. Fleas flies and fish are fantastic frog food.

4. Joan jumps in January jogs in June and enjoys jigsaw puzzles in July.

5. The knight knows how to kneel knock and knit.

6. Is it Indiana Illinois Idaho or Iowa in that interesting illustration?

7. Peter picks petunias peonies and pansies.

Write your own sentences, making most of the words begin with the given letter.
Include three or more words in a series that need to be separated with commas.
You can use a dictionary for ideas.

B _____

_____

M _____

_____

A _____

_____

T _____

_____

What'll We Do?

Use an **apostrophe** (') in a contraction to show one or more letters are missing.
can't can not   *o'clock of the clock*   *what's what is*

Use an **apostrophe** (') with a noun to show possession.
Tiffany's pen   *the students' desks*   *the children's books*

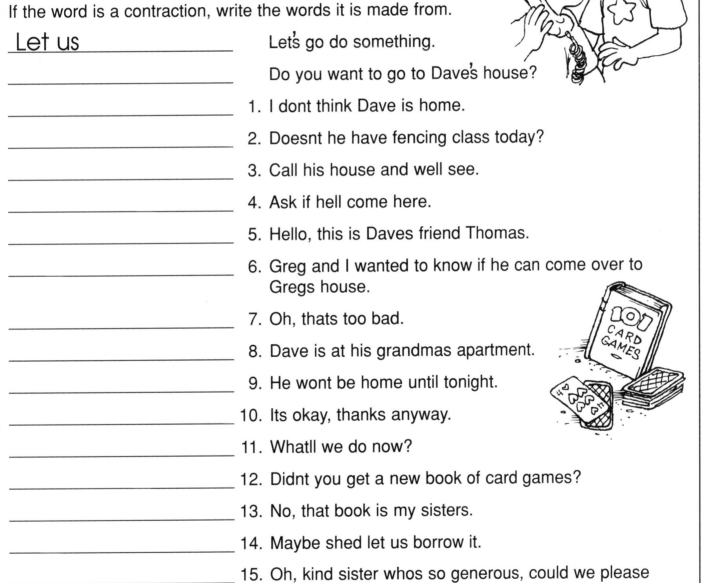

Read each sentence. Add the missing apostrophe.
If the word is a contraction, write the words it is made from.

Let us _____

_____

_____

_____

_____

_____

_____

_____

_____

_____

_____

_____

_____

_____

_____

Let's go do something.

Do you want to go to Dave's house?

1. I dont think Dave is home.

2. Doesnt he have fencing class today?

3. Call his house and well see.

4. Ask if hell come here.

5. Hello, this is Daves friend Thomas.

6. Greg and I wanted to know if he can come over to Gregs house.

7. Oh, thats too bad.

8. Dave is at his grandmas apartment.

9. He wont be home until tonight.

10. Its okay, thanks anyway.

11. Whatll we do now?

12. Didnt you get a new book of card games?

13. No, that book is my sisters.

14. Maybe shed let us borrow it.

15. Oh, kind sister whos so generous, could we please borrow your book of card games?

Dear **A**esop

Proofread this letter. Check off (✔) each step as you do it.

- ☐ Underline three times the 8 letters that should be capitalized. (i̲)
- ☐ Write the 4 missing periods. (.)
- ☐ Write the 2 missing question marks. (**?**)
- ☐ Write the 3 missing commas. (,)
- ☐ Write the 2 missing apostrophes. (')
- ☐ Write the 1 missing set of quotation marks. (" ")

april 1   2003

dear Aesop

Why did you have to make up that foolish story "The Tortoise and the Hare"   I am so tired of it   The hares in my family have always been speed champions.   look at how we are built   My long feet and powerful back legs are a work of art!   yet every time a child hears your story, I lose the race to a poky tortoise.   Its not fair!

Couldnt you have made the story "Aesop and the tortoise" or "The Cheetah and the Hare"   Then maybe my dear mom wouldn't say to me,   That Aesop is a terrible storyteller.

Instead i spend my life hopping from library to library, adding pages to books so that I win the race

I must go now.   I need to write a letter to Ms. beatrix Potter Thank you for your time.

yours truly

Hare

Answer Key

Page 8
Sentences will vary. Underlined sentence fragments:
1. So cute!
2. Are very good swimmers and divers.
3. Many different kinds of penguins.
4. Only weigh about two pounds.
5. Then see my favorite birds.

Page 9
Sentences will vary.

Page 10
Subjects and predicates will vary.

Page 11
1. We; We
2. program; That program
3. group; One group of kids
4. group; Another group
5. group; The group I was in
6. Kids; Kids in all the different classes
7. class; Our class
8. parents; Our parents
9. We; We
10. people; The people at Community Food Share
11. They; They
12. class; Our class

Page 12
1. made; made . . . mummies.
2. drew; drew . . . cats.
3. wrote; wrote . . . details.
4. wore; wore . . . party.
5. had; had . . . wigs.
6. wore; wore makeup.
7. put; put . . . Egyptian.
8. read; read . . . Cleopatra.
9. acted; acted . . . parts.
10. needed; needed . . . Antony.
11. brought; brought . . . hieroglyphics.
12. are; are . . . writing.
13. stamped; stamped . . . paper.
14. were; were . . . then.
15. snacked; snacked . . . Egyptian!
16. went; finally . . . a.m.

Page 13
1. Marco and Kelsey will demonstrate yo-yo tricks.
2. Laura is teaching how to dribble and pass a soccer ball.
3. Todd will bring his skates and helmet.
4. Ryan and Maggie are making up games about famous athletes.

Page 14
Sentences will vary.

Page 15
Sentences will vary.

Page 16
Sentences will vary.

Page 17
1. Q ?
2. C .
3. S .
4. Q ?
5. C .
6. C . (or E !)
7. E !
8. Q ?
9. S .
10. C .
11. S .
12. E !
13. Q ?
14. S .
15. C .

Page 28
Nouns and stories will vary.

Page 29
Possible abstract nouns: citizenship, connection, exploration, freedom, friendship, happiness, illness, information, kindness, kingdom, kingship, pollution, punishment, statement, wisdom, wiseness

Page 30
Proper nouns will vary.

Page 31

```
s h e e p b z w o m e n m k y
c o w c o o x e n e e o o i t
l u q h p x - r a y s u m s o
e m m i c e     a z n f s y
a p p l e s     r a s h e s
v i a d o g s   d q f a s v
e r r r u i z o o s u e n l a
s e t e q u e e n s a e d i s
x s i n c h e s s w i t s s e
n o e l v e s z j e l l i e s
b u s e s g r a p e s k a t y
```

apples   nouns
boxes   oxen
children   parties
dogs   queens
elves   rashes
feet   sheep
grapes   toys
hands   umpires
inches   vases
jellies   women
kisses   x-rays
leaves   yards
mice   zoos

Page 32
1. boy's toys; boys' toys
2. snakes' aches; snake's aches
3. teacher's bleachers; teachers' bleachers
4. pigs' twigs; pig's twigs
5. grandmother's brothers; grandmothers' brothers
6. man's crayons; men's pens

Page 33
1. Shakespeare—He
2. Ms. Meyer—She
3. the class—we
4. The chorus—They
5. Kristen—She
6. Mike—He
7. The class—We
8. The co-leaders—They
9. The performance—It
10. Ms. Meyer—I
11. The class—You

Page 34
1. Ashley's dad—him
2. the bowl—it
3. Ashley and her dad—us
4. Ashley's grandma—her
5. the bulbs—them
6. Ashley—me
7. the bulbs—them
8. Ashley—me
9. the blooming—it
10. Ashley—you
11. Ashley's dad—me
12. Ashley and her dad—you

Page 35
Action verbs will vary.

Page 36
Sentences will vary. Verbs:
1. is   7. Is
2. am   8. Are
3. are   9. Are
4. is   10. Are
5. are   11. Is
6. is   12. Am

3123303 Grammar Made Simple Grade 4 ■ © Frank Schaffer Publications, Inc.

Page 37
Additional verbs will vary.

kicked	wagged
gathered	hummed
looked	skipped
played	rubbed
answered	clapped
liked	tried
raced	multiplied
smiled	studied
dribbled	hurried
shared	married

Page 39

1. was making
2. had assigned
3. wrote
4. started
5. drew
6. do like
7. saw
8. was shaking
9. could believe
10. were moving
11. turned
12. Would help
13. did say
14. am trapped
15. called
16. is talking
17. came
18. did move
19. should go
20. nodded

Page 40
Adjectives and illustrations will vary.

Page 41

quiet	quieter	quietest
cautious	more cautious	most cautious
tall	taller	tallest
bright	brighter	brightest
beautiful	more beautiful	most beautiful
strong	stronger	strongest
spirited	more spirited	most spirited
late	later	latest
funny	funnier	funniest
nice	nicer	nicest
generous	more generous	most generous
Answers vary.		

Page 42
Adverbs will vary.

Page 43
The dog is <u>on</u> the rug, <u>under</u> the table, <u>next to</u> the cat.
The tennis shoes are <u>in</u> the closet, <u>on</u> the floor, <u>between</u> the boots and the sandals.
The queen is <u>in</u> the dining hall, <u>at</u> the table, <u>with</u> the prince.

The balloon is floating <u>in</u> the sky, <u>above</u> our heads, far <u>from</u> our reach.

Page 48

1. makes
2. hear
3. warn
4. make
5. emits
6. bounce
7. use
8. make
9. listens
10. sing
11. hears
12. hunt
13. helps
14. hears

Page 49
My name is Zippisplat. I am an alien. I come from the planet Splat. It is far, far away from Earth. Splat is a wonderful planet.

I am visiting Earth for one month. My family is not here with me. They are still on Splat. I miss them very much. I even miss my little brother. He is sometimes a brat, but I love him.

I am happy to be here because Earthlings are very friendly.

Page 50

1. was—were
2. found—finded
3. thought—thinked
4. had seen—seen
5. said—say
6. chose—choosed
7. wrote—writed
8. said—sayed
9. added—add
10. made—maked
11. had—haved
12. kept—keeped
13. won—winned
14. turned—turn
15. let—letted

Page 51

1. kids
2. dessert
3. recipes
4. pictures
5. pie
6. recipe
7. ingredients
8. apples
9. trees
10. crust
11. cookies
12. egg
13. balls
14. desserts
15. sign
16. people
17. leftovers

Page 52
Names will vary. They should precede the pronoun.

1. me
2. I
3. me
4. I
5. me
6. I
7. me
8. I
9. I
10. me
11. I
12. me

Page 53
. . . My aunt gave it to <u>me</u> . . . <u>She</u> told me . . . and like <u>it</u> a lot. Some of <u>them</u> are free . . .
. . . First <u>I</u> wrote . . . I had to write <u>it</u> very neatly . . . If you don't remember the envelope, the place might not send <u>you</u> your stuff . . . Then <u>I</u> waited some more.
. . . I asked <u>him</u> . . . I quickly opened <u>it</u> up. The Tigers sent <u>me</u> . . . <u>They</u> gave . . .
The next letter <u>I</u> wrote was to m aunt. I thanked <u>her</u> for my book.
. . . <u>We</u> will . . .

Page 54

1. an
2. a
3. a
4. a
5. an
6. a
7. an
8. a
9. an
10. an
11. a
12. a
13. a
14. a
15. an
16. an
17. a
18. an
19. a
20. an
21. an
22. a
23. a
24. a
25. a
26. an
27. a
28. a
29. an
30. a
31. an
32. a
33. a
34. an
35. a
36. a
37. a
38. a

Page 55

1. fast
2. faster
3. fastest
4. slow
5. good
6. best
7. larger
8. largest
9. huge
10. tiny
11. tinier
12. protective
13. more ferocious
14. better
15. heavy

FS123303 Grammar Made Simple Grade 4 ▪ © Frank Schaffer Publications, In

Page 56

1. Their
2. your
3. It's
4. You're
5. your
6. They're
7. their
8. its
9. It's
10. You're
11. their
12. it's
13. your
14. You're
15. your
16. They're
17. It's
18. Its

Page 57

1. New
2. one
3. wants
4. in
5. to
6. It's
7. too
8. read
9. see
10. where
11. for
12. would
13. border
14. know

Page 63

These nouns should have the first letter underlined three times:
national, wyoming, montana, idaho, ant, yellowstone, lake, michael, d, faithful, roosevelt, lodge, teddy, oosevelt, yellowstone

Paragraphs will vary.

Page 64

Students should have underlined the marked letters three times:

may 2, 2003

ear busy beaver,

i would be happy to help you. ease do not wait until thursday. ome as soon as you can. my ddress is 123 w. animal drive.

your friend,
dr. doolittle

Thank-you notes will vary.

Page 65

Doctor — Mrs.
December — Mr.
Monday — Dec.
Mistress — Dr.
Mister — Sr.
January — Mon.
Junior — Ave.
Senior — Jr.
Street — Jan.
Avenue — Rd.
Boulevard — St.
Road — Blvd.

February — Fr.
Friday — Feb.
Father — Fri.
Reverend — Sept.
Saint — St.
September — Rev.
inch(es) — ft.
foot/feet — lb.
yard(s) — mi.
mile(s) — in.
ounce(s) — oz.
pound(s) — yd.

1. Martin Luther King, Jr.
2. St. Louis, Missouri
3. Peña Blvd.
4. Dr. McCandless
5. State St.
6. Mr. Thomas A. Edison
7. Feb. 14th
8. Pennsylvania Ave.
9. Mrs. Eleanor Roosevelt
10. 7 lb.

Page 66

Have you . . . day**?** Yesterday was . . . life**!** *(or .)* I made . . . recital**.**

I like . . . lessons**.** My piano . . . helpful**.** Twice a . . . recital**.** Each student . . . well**.**

A month ago my piano teacher had asked, "What song . . . Dennis**?**"

"Could I play *Für Elise***?**" I asked.

"Certainly!" she exclaimed. "That would . . . you**.**"

Für Elise . . . Beethoven**.** I practiced . . . again**.** I could . . . home**.**

My parents . . . recital**.** When I . . . nervous**.** He plays . . . band**.** What would . . . me**?**

When it . . . audience**.** What a crowd! Instead of . . . softly**.** I hit . . . another**.** Finally it was over**.** I stood . . . red**.**

After the . . . dessert**.** My granddad . . . mood**.** "What's wrong**?**" he asked.

"I played horribly**!** *(or .)* "

He said, "Every musician . . . then**.**"

"What do . . . Granddad**?**" I asked him.

"I pretend . . . audience," he answered. "Try it next time**.**"

Page 67

"We get to do yo-yos in gym today," announced Rebecca.

"Did you bring a yo-yo?" asked Jake.

"Yes, I brought the new one I got for my birthday," answered Rebecca.

Nathan chimed in, "I don't have one."

"Don't worry," said Rebecca. "Ms. James has yo-yos for everybody."

Nathan asked, "Do you know any tricks?"

"I can do Walk the Dog," said Jake. "Watch!"

"Wow! That's cool!" exclaimed Nathan and Rebecca.

"I am learning Rock the Baby," said Rebecca. "I'll show you."

"That was pretty good," said Nathan.

"I can do it better," said Rebecca. "Let me try it again."

"Hey, you did it!" shouted Jake. "That was great."

Page 68

"I brought you this basket of goodies," said Red Riding Hood.

"Your hand, er, I mean the basket, looks quite tasty," replied the Wolf. "Thank you, dear."

Red Riding Hood asked, "Grandmother, would you like me to read you a story?"

"That would be lovely," said the Wolf.

"I'll sit here in this rocking chair," said Red Riding Hood.

"Please come sit on my bed, dear," pleaded the Wolf, "so I may hear you better."

"With those big ears, you could hear me at my home," mumbled Red Riding Hood.

"Watch it, smart aleck!" exclaimed the Wolf, grabbing Red Riding Hood.

"Let me go!" shouted Red Riding Hood.

"The only place you are going is inside me," said the Wolf cruelly.

Red Riding Hood quickly squirmed out of the Wolf's grasp and asked, "Where is my grandmother?"

Page 69
1. Christopher . . . October 12, 1492.
2. The largest. . . Mexico City, Mexico.
3. Many . . . in Montreal, Canada.
4. You . . . visit Granada, Nicaragua.
5. Delaware . . . December 7, 1787.
6. Hawaii . . . August 21, 1959.
7. The highest . . . Death Valley, California.
8. The lowest . . . at Northice, Greenland.
9. Several . . . September 15, 1821.
10. The Mississippi . . . New Orleans, Louisiana.
11. The Battle. . . June 25, 1876.
12. The sun . . . Point Barrow, Alaska.
13. On December 17, 1903, . . . airplane.
14. Canada's . . . February 15, 1965.
15. The world's . . . in Chicago, Illinois.
16. Many . . . Montego Bay, Jamaica.

Page 70
Students should have written a comma in the date, at the end of the greeting, and at the end of the closing:

        July 28, 2004
Dear Ms. Spider,
        Your acquaintance,

The reply letters will vary.

Page 71
1. Adam, what did the mayonnaise say to the refrigerator?
    I don't know, Bonnie, what?
Close the door, I'm dressing!

2. Larry, where do cows go for fun?
    To a playground?
No, to the moo-vies!

3. Jessica, where do sheep get their hair cut?
    I don't know, Daniel.
    At a hair salon?
At the baa-baa shop!
    Ugh, I should have known that!

4. Bobby, what animals like to write letters?
    Snakes?
No, pigs.
    I don't get it, Kim.
They're pen pals!

5. Melanie, do you know any riddles?
    Yes, I do, Miss Anthony.
    What is black and white and red all over?
A newspaper?
    No, an embarrassed zebra!

Page 72
1. Otis ordered oysters, oranges, olives, or oatmeal.
2. Will Wanda wait for William, Winston, and Winifred?
3. Fleas, flies, and fish are fantastic frog food.
4. Joan jumps in January, jogs in June, and enjoys jigsaw puzzles in July.
5. The knight knows how to kneel, knock, and knit.
6. Is it Indiana, Illinois, Idaho, or Iowa in that interesting illustration?
7. Peter picks petunias, peonies, and pansies.
Sentences will vary.

Page 73
1. do not—don't
2. Does not—Doesn't
3. we will—we'll
4. he will—he'll
5. Dave's
6. Greg's
7. that is—that's
8. grandma's
9. will not—won't
10. It is—It's
11. What will—What'll
12. Did not—Didn't
13. sister's
14. she would—she'd
15. who is—who's

Page 74
Students should have underlined the marked letters three times:
    <u>a</u>pril 1, 2003
<u>d</u>ear Aesop,
    Why did you have to mak<u>e</u> up that foolish story "The Tortoise and the Hare"**?** I am so tired of it The hares in my family have alwa<u>y</u> been speed champions. <u>l</u>ook at how we are built**.** My long feet an<u>d</u> powerful back legs are a work of art! <u>y</u>et every time a child hears your story, I lose the race to a po<u>k</u>y tortoise. It's not fair!
    Couldn't you have made the story "Aesop and the <u>t</u>ortoise" or "The Cheetah and the Hare"**?** Then maybe my dear mom would say to me, "That Aesop is a terrib<u>l</u>e storyteller."
    Instead <u>i</u> spend my life hopping from library to library, adding pages to books so that I w<u>in</u> the race**.**
    I must go now. I need to write a letter to Ms. <u>b</u>eatrix Potter**.** Thank you for your time.
        <u>y</u>ours truly,
        Hare

FS123303 Grammar Made Simple Grade 4 ▪ © Frank Schaffer Publications, In